FOOD, FOOTBALL, AND FUN!

SPORTS ILLUSTRATED KIDS' FOOTBALL RECIPES

BY KATRINA JORGENSEN

capstone
young readers

TABLE OF CONTENTS

Score With Your Football Party!

Ready to make the big play? Set the menu for your football party, tailgating outing, or game day nutrition. Team up any of the appetizers, main courses, desserts, and drinks to make the perfect formation. Get started by gathering the supplies and ingredients. See each recipe for the full list of what you'll need to start cooking.

PREP TIME	the amount of time it takes to prepare ingredients before cooking
INACTIVE PREP TIME	the amount of time it takes to indirectly prepare ingredients before cooking, such as allowing dough to rise
COOK TIME	the amount of time it takes to cook a recipe after preparing the ingredients

Conversions

Using metric tools? No problem! These metric conversions will make your recipe measure up.

Temperature

Fahrenheit	Celsius
325°	160°
350°	180°
375°	190°
400°	200°
425°	220°
450°	230°

Measurements

¼ teaspoon	1.25 grams or milliliters
½ teaspoon	2.5 g or mL
1 teaspoon	5 g or mL
1 tablespoon	15 g or mL
¼ cup	57 g (dry) or 60 mL (liquid)
⅓ cup	75 g (dry) or 80 mL (liquid)
½ cup	114 g (dry) or 125 mL (liquid)
⅔ cup	150 g (dry) or 160 mL (liquid)
¾ cup	170 g (dry) or 175 mL (liquid)
1 cup	227 g (dry) or 240 mL (liquid)
1 quart	950 mL

blend—to mix together, sometimes using a blender

boil—to heat until large bubbles form on top of a liquid; the boiling point for water is 212°F (100°C)

chop—to cut into small pieces with a knife

dissolve—to incorporate a solid food into a liquid by melting or stirring

grate—to cut into small strips using a grater

knead—to mix dough by flattening it with the heel of your hand, folding it in half, pressing down again, and repeating several times; use flour on your work surface to prevent the dough from sticking

mash—to smash a soft food into a lumpy mixture

preheat—to turn the oven on ahead of time so it reaches the correct temperature before you are ready to bake

simmer—to cook foods in hot liquids kept just below the boiling point of water

slice—to cut into thin pieces with a knife

spread—to put a thin layer of a soft food onto another food

thaw—to bring frozen food to room temperature

Keep your eye open for helpful, creative, and informative sidebars throughout the book. Switch up your recipes with Call an Audible ideas, and get insight from the expert with Coach's Tips. Athlete Nutrition highlights valuable nutrient information to explain why certain foods are good for you—the athlete.

Follow the coach's advice on how to cut an onion (page 63) or a bell pepper (page 105).

CALL AN AUDIBLE

Not liking what you see at the start of the play? Make some changes in the recipe to have success against even the toughest defenses.

COACH'S TIP

Gain the edge in the kitchen with these cool tips, tricks, and techniques.

ATHLETE NUTRITION

Fuel up on information about the vitamins and nutrients you need to storm the field.

Tailgating Tips

The tailgating recipes in this book can either be made at home or finished at the game. Steps numbered in orange highlight what you need to do to finish the big play at the stadium.

Safety in the Kitchen

You can have fun in the kitchen and be safe too. Always start your recipes with clean hands, tools, and surfaces. Make sure you wash your hands and keep your tools and surfaces clean after handling raw meat. Use your knife carefully. Ask an adult for help when cutting food or handling hot dishes.

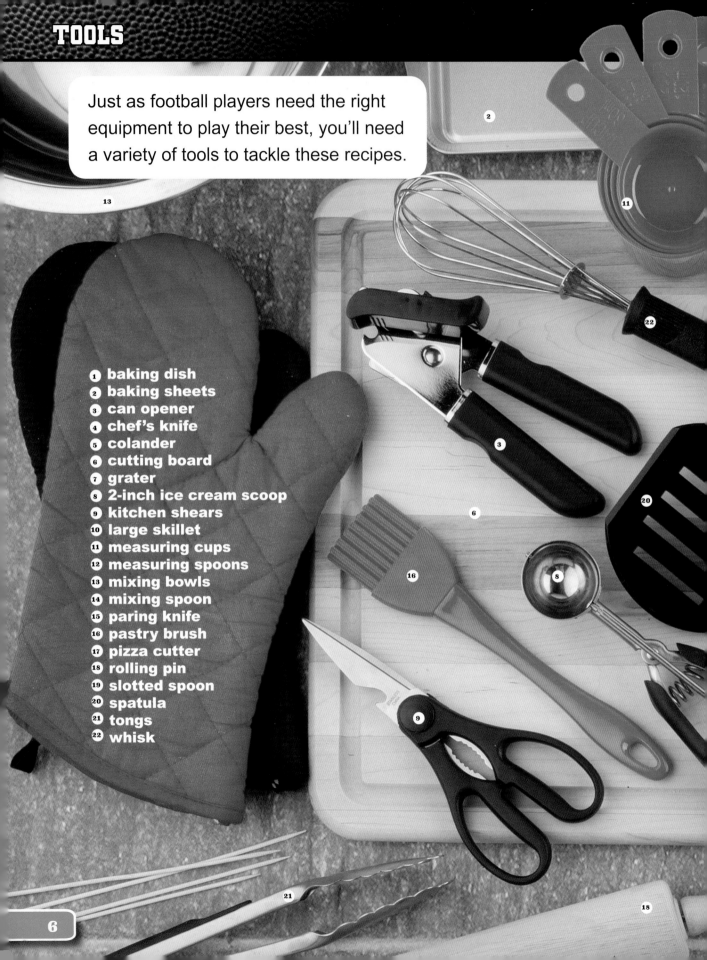

Just as football players need the right equipment to play their best, you'll need a variety of tools to tackle these recipes.

1. baking dish
2. baking sheets
3. can opener
4. chef's knife
5. colander
6. cutting board
7. grater
8. 2-inch ice cream scoop
9. kitchen shears
10. large skillet
11. measuring cups
12. measuring spoons
13. mixing bowls
14. mixing spoon
15. paring knife
16. pastry brush
17. pizza cutter
18. rolling pin
19. slotted spoon
20. spatula
21. tongs
22. whisk

SOFT PRETZEL BITES
AND HONEY-MUSTARD DIPPING SAUCE

Delicious bite-sized pretzels are sure to score a touchdown with your crowd.

PREP TIME	**1 HOUR** (½ HOUR INACTIVE)
COOK TIME	**30 MINUTES** (INACTIVE)
MAKES	**ABOUT 32 PRETZEL BITES**

Tools

- measuring spoons
- 3 saucepans
- 3 mixing bowls
- measuring cups
- damp kitchen towel
- chef's knife
- kitchen shears
- baking sheet
- parchment paper
- slotted spoon
- pastry brush

Ingredients

For the dough:

- 2 tablespoons butter
- 1 packet instant yeast
- 1 pinch of salt
- 1 teaspoon honey
- 1 cup warm water
- 2½ cups flour, plus more for kneading
- vegetable oil spray

For cooking:

- 3 cups water
- ½ cup baking soda
- vegetable oil spray
- 6 tablespoons butter
- kosher salt, for sprinkling
- poppy seeds, for sprinkling
- sesame seeds, for sprinkling

For the honey-mustard dip:

- 1 cup coarse ground mustard
- ½ cup honey
- 1 teaspoon salt

1 Place 2 tablespoons butter in a saucepan and melt over low heat.

2 In a large mixing bowl, combine the butter, yeast, salt, honey, and warm water. Allow to sit for about 2 minutes.

3 Add the flour. Mix it well and turn the bowl upside down onto a floured surface. Knead the dough well with your hands for about 5 minutes, or until it is soft and smooth.

4 Spray the inside of a clean mixing bowl with vegetable oil spray and place the dough in the bowl. Cover with a clean damp cloth and allow to sit for 30 minutes to rise.

COACH'S TIP

What's in a "pinch?" There is no spoon to measure this tiny amount. Whatever you can grab between your thumb and forefinger is the perfect measurement.

5   Flour your surface again and place the dough ball on it. Knead for one minute and then cut the dough into six equal pieces.

6   Roll the dough between your hands and the counter to make ropes about 12 inches long.

7   Using kitchen shears, snip each rope into 12 equal pieces.

8   Preheat oven to 400°F. Line baking sheet with parchment paper and set aside.

9   Boil the water in a saucepan. Add baking soda and stir until it dissolves. Reduce the heat so it slowly simmers.

10 Drop the dough bites in the saucepan six at a time. Let them cook for about 30 seconds.

11 Remove the dough bites from the pan with a slotted spoon. Place the bites about ¼-inch apart on the baking sheet. Sprinkle with salt. Add seeds for extra flavor if desired.

12 Bake for about 15 minutes or until they are golden brown.

13 Meanwhile, melt 6 tablespoons butter in a saucepan over low heat.

14 Remove from oven and brush with melted butter using the pastry brush. Allow to cool for about 10 minutes before serving.

CALL AN AUDIBLE

Switch from savory to sweet by sprinkling your pretzel bites with cinnamon and sugar instead of salt.

For the dipping sauce:

1   Combine all of the ingredients in the mixing bowl.

2   Taste the mixture and add more honey or mustard if needed. Serve alongside your pretzel bites.

SWEET & SALTY SNACK MIX

Nuts and pretzels come together with sweet and salty flavors for a pregame snack.

PREP TIME	10 MINUTES
COOK TIME	15 MINUTES
MAKES	ABOUT 4 CUPS

Tools

- large baking sheet
- parchment paper
- measuring cups/ spoons
- small saucepan
- large mixing bowl
- bowl scraper

Ingredients

- 1 tablespoon butter
- ¼ cup water
- ½ cup sugar
- ¾ teaspoon salt
- ½ teaspoon pepper
- 2 cups mixed nuts, unsalted
- 2 cups pretzels

1. Preheat oven to 350°F. Line a baking sheet with parchment paper and set aside.

2. In the saucepan, combine the butter, water, and sugar. Place over medium heat. Stir to dissolve the sugar and simmer for 1 minute. Set aside.

3. Combine the remaining ingredients in the mixing bowl.

4. Slowly pour the butter, water, and sugar over the nut mixture and stir gently with your bowl scraper. Be careful not to break the pretzels.

5. Pour the nut mixture onto the baking sheet. Carefully spread the mixture out into a single layer.

6. Bake for 10 minutes. Then remove from the oven and stir the nut mixture, keeping it in a single layer.

7. Bake an additional 5 minutes. Allow to cool for 15 minutes before serving.

CALL AN AUDIBLE

Want to spice up the recipe? Add ½ teaspoon cayenne pepper and 1 teaspoon cumin in step 2.

FOOTBALL BACON CHEESEBALL

Before the game's opening kickoff, you can kick off your party with a cheesy appetizer.

PREP TIME	25 MINUTES
COOK TIME	2 HOURS (INACTIVE)
SERVES	6 TO 8 PEOPLE

Tools

- large skillet
- tongs
- paper towels
- chef's knife
- cutting board
- large mixing bowl
- measuring cups
- grater
- bowl scraper
- plastic wrap
- serving plate

Ingredients

- 8 ounces bacon
- 4 ounces white cheddar cheese
- 3 green onions
- 8 ounces cream cheese, at room temperature
- 1 teaspoon pepper
- crackers, chips, and veggies for serving

1. Place bacon in skillet over medium heat and cook until crispy on both sides, using tongs to flip. Be careful of spatters!

2. Set the cooked bacon on a small stack of paper towels to drain extra fat. Allow to cool for 10 minutes.

3. Coarsely chop bacon into bite-sized pieces and place half in the mixing bowl. Set the rest aside.

CALL AN AUDIBLE

Not a fan of bacon? Sub in 2 cups of chopped pecans instead. Skip steps 1 and 2, and mix in half the pecans in step 3. Use the remaining half to cover the cheeseball in step 8.

4. Cut one slice of the white cheddar cheese and set aside. Grate the rest and place in the mixing bowl.

5. Chop the green onions finely and add to mixing bowl.

6. In the mixing bowl, add cream cheese and pepper. Mix well with bowl scraper.

7. Scrape the cheese mixture onto a large sheet of plastic wrap. Using the plastic to avoid getting your hands cheesy, shape the mixture into a round ball.

8. Refrigerate the plastic-wrapped ball for 2 hours.

9. While the ball is still in the plastic, form into a football shape the best you can. Remove the plastic and place on a serving plate.

10. Cover the cheeseball with the remaining bacon.

11. Remember the slice of white cheddar cheese you set aside in step 4? Cut that piece into small slices for the laces. Place on the cheeseball.

12. Serve with a variety of crackers, vegetables, and chips.

PEACH BBQ MEATBALLS

Deliciously sweet and tangy, these meatballs are a snap to make and sure to be a party pleaser!

PREP TIME	**45** MINUTES
COOK TIME	**4 HOURS** (INACTIVE)
MAKES	ABOUT **25** 2-INCH MEATBALLS

Tools

- 1-quart saucepan
- measuring cups
- mixing spoon
- large mixing bowl
- measuring spoons
- fork
- 2-inch scoop
- 2 baking sheets
- 10-inch skillet
- tongs
- 3-quart slow cooker

Ingredients

- 1 pound lean ground beef
- 1 pound ground pork
- 2 eggs
- 1 cup bread crumbs
- ½ cup milk
- 1 teaspoon garlic powder
- 1 teaspoon onion powder
- 1½ teaspoons salt
- 1 teaspoon pepper
- pinch red pepper flakes
- 2 tablespoons oil

For the sauce:

- 24-ounce bottle of your favorite barbecue sauce
- 8-ounce jar peach preserves

1. In the saucepan, combine the barbecue sauce and peach preserves. Over medium heat, stir the sauce until it begins to simmer. Remove from heat and set aside.

2. In a large mixing bowl, combine beef, pork, eggs, bread crumbs, milk, garlic powder, onion powder, salt, pepper, and red pepper flakes.

3. Mash the mixture with a fork to combine the ingredients. You can use your hands too!

4. Using the 2-inch scoop, portion out scoops of the meat mixture onto the first baking sheet.

5. Shape them into balls by rolling them in a circular pattern between your palms. Place them back on the baking sheet.

6. Heat the oil in a skillet over medium heat. Add a handful of meatballs with about 1 inch of space between each one. Carefully brown all sides of the meatballs. Use tongs to place them on the second, clean baking sheet. Finish browning the remaining meatballs in batches if necessary. Don't worry if they aren't cooked inside. They will finish cooking in the slow cooker.

7 Turn the slow cooker on low. Place the meatballs in the slow cooker and pour the prepared sauce over them. Stir gently until all the meatballs are coated.

8 Cook covered for about 4 hours. Stir occasionally.

9 Place the meatballs on a platter and serve.

COACH'S TIP

Help your guests to avoid fumbling the meatballs! Poke toothpicks or mini skewers in each one to make them easy to grab.

FRESH FRUIT SALAD

Bring some color to your football party with a roster full of your favorite fruits.

PREP TIME — 20 MINUTES

COOK TIME — 5 TO 10 MINUTES

SERVES — 6 PEOPLE

Tools

- measuring cups/spoons
- saucepan
- spoon
- chef's knife
- cutting board
- 2 mixing bowls

Ingredients

- ½ cup pineapple juice
- 1 teaspoon vanilla extract
- 3 cups strawberries
- 1 cup red grapes
- 1 cup blueberries
- 1 cup pineapple
- 1 15-ounce can mandarin oranges, drained

COACH'S TIP

Don't let your fruit salad get dried out! Be sure to cover it and keep it in a refrigerator until you're ready to serve.

1 In a saucepan over medium heat, add the pineapple juice and vanilla extract. Heat until it begins to simmer, then reduce heat to medium-low. Allow the liquid to reduce by half. The liquid should begin to thicken like syrup after about 5 to 10 minutes.

2 Meanwhile, chop the strawberries and pineapple into bite-sized pieces and place in a mixing bowl with the grapes and blueberries.

3 Transfer the syrup to a small mixing bowl and place in the refrigerator for about 10 minutes or until cooled.

4 Pour cooled syrup over the fruit and toss gently to coat.

Dips are the perfect addition to your bowl party. Your party guests will be lining up to spike their crackers, chips, and veggies into your variety of dips.

GARLICKY HUMMUS

PREP TIME	20 MINUTES
SERVES	6 TO 8 PEOPLE

Tools

- colander
- measuring cups
- food processor
- bowl scraper
- cutting board
- chef's knife

Ingredients

- 2 15-ounce cans chickpeas (garbanzo beans)
- 2 lemons
- ½ cup tahini sauce (sesame seed paste)
- 2 cloves garlic
- 1 teaspoon paprika
- 1 teaspoon salt
- ¼ cup olive oil
- ¼ cup water

1 Drain the chickpeas in a colander and run cool water over them to rinse.

2 Place half of the chickpeas in the food processor and turn on high for 30 seconds.

3 Scrape the edges of the food processor bowl with a bowl scraper so that the chickpeas are at the bottom of the bowl again. Add remaining chickpeas and turn the food processor back on high for an additional 30 seconds.

4 Slice the lemons in half and squeeze the juice directly into the food processor. Catch the seeds if they fall out by holding your hand under the stream of juice.

5 Add remaining ingredients and turn the food processor on high until the mixture is smooth.

6 If the hummus seems a little thick, add 1 tablespoon of water at a time until it is as thick or thin as you prefer.

7 Scrape the hummus into a serving bowl. Serve with pita chips and sliced bell peppers.

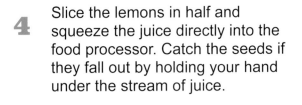

COACH'S TIP

Don't have a food processor? No problem. A large blender will work too. To make sure you don't give the blender more than it can handle, do steps 2 and 3 in smaller batches.

FAST AND FRESH SALSA

PREP TIME	**20** MINUTES

COOK TIME	**1** HOUR (INACTIVE)

SERVES	**6** TO **8** PEOPLE

Tools

- chef's knife
- cutting board
- measuring spoons
- large mixing bowl
- spoon

Ingredients

- **4 Roma tomatoes**
- **1 small red onion**
- **1 jalapeño**
- **½ bunch cilantro**
- **1 teaspoon honey**
- **1 teaspoon salt**
- **1 teaspoon cumin**

1 Chop the tomatoes and red onion. Place in mixing bowl.

2 Seed and slice the jalapeño by slicing lengthwise and scooping the insides firmly with a spoon. Discard seeds. Chop the jalapeño and add to mixing bowl.

3 Pull the leaves off the stems of the cilantro. Don't worry if a few stems end up with the leaves. Push into a small pile and chop into very small pieces.

4 Add remaining ingredients and stir to combine.

5 Allow to stand at room temperature for 1 hour before serving with tortilla chips.

COACH'S TIP

Don't touch your eyes or face when handling hot peppers like jalapeños! They contain a chemical that may cause a burning sensation. Be sure to wash your hands well when you're done.

GREAT GUACAMOLE

Tools

- chef's knife
- cutting board
- kitchen towel
- spoon
- large mixing bowl
- fork
- measuring spoons

Ingredients

- 4 ripe avocados
- 2 limes
- ½ bunch cilantro, chopped
- 1 teaspoon salt
- 1 teaspoon pepper
- 1 clove garlic, minced

1 Have an adult cut the avocados in half and remove the pits. Remove the pits by holding one half in your hand and tapping the blade of the chef's knife on the pit, and then gently twist. Remove the pit from the knife, using a kitchen towel to guard your hand from cuts.

2 Use a spoon to scoop out the avocado flesh from the skin and place it in a large mixing bowl.

3 Slice the limes in half and squeeze the juice into the mixing bowl.

4 Add the remaining ingredients.

5 Use the fork to lightly mash the avocado until it is well blended with the other ingredients.

6 Optional: Add 1 cup of the Fast and Fresh Salsa for additional flavor.

7 Cover the bowl and place in the refrigerator for 1 hour before serving. Serve with tortilla chips and a wedge of lime.

KICKIN' THREE-BEAN CHILI

Not one, not two, but three kinds of beans give this chili a party-winning kick.

PREP TIME	20 MINUTES
COOK TIME	1 HOUR
SERVES	8 PEOPLE

Tools

- cutting board
- chef's knife
- stockpot
- mixing spoon
- measuring spoons
- can opener

Ingredients

- 1 tablespoon oil
- 2 bell peppers, chopped
- 2 onions, chopped
- 1 jalapeño, seeds removed and chopped
- 2 pounds lean ground beef
- 2 tablespoons cumin
- ¼ cup chili powder
- 1 teaspoon oregano
- 1 teaspoon paprika
- 1 teaspoon salt
- 1 teaspoon pepper
- ¼ teaspoon cayenne pepper
- 2 15-ounce cans fire-roasted tomatoes, undrained
- 1 15-ounce can black beans, drained
- 1 15-ounce can kidney beans, drained
- 1 15-ounce can pinto beans, drained

Garnishes:
- shredded cheese
- sour cream
- chopped green onions
- crushed tortilla chips

CALL AN AUDIBLE

Want to make this recipe vegetarian? Instead of ground beef, add 2 cups of chopped zucchini, 2 cups of chopped carrots, and 1 cup of chopped eggplant. Reduce the cooking time to 30 minutes.

1 Heat oil over medium heat in a stockpot.

2 Add peppers, onions, and jalapeño to the stockpot and stir. Cook for about 5 minutes, stirring occasionally.

3 Add ground beef and break it up with a mixing spoon. Cook until no longer pink, about 5 to 8 minutes, while stirring occasionally. With an adult's help, drain the fat carefully.

4 Add cumin, chili powder, oregano, paprika, salt, pepper, and cayenne pepper to the pot and stir. Cook for 1 minute.

5 Add tomatoes and beans. Stir all of the ingredients and then reduce heat to medium-low.

6 Simmer for 1 hour. Serve hot in bowls with garnishes.

TANGY BBQ CHICKEN QUESADILLAS

For a barbecue flavor that will tackle your taste buds, try sweet and tangy chicken quesadillas.

PREP TIME	**45** MINUTES
COOK TIME	**20** MINUTES
SERVES	**6 TO 8 PEOPLE**

Tools

- 2 baking sheets
- parchment paper
- cutting board
- chef's knife
- 2 skillets
- measuring cup/ spoons
- spatula
- small mixing bowl
- spoon

Ingredients

- 2 boneless, skinless chicken breasts
- ½ teaspoon salt
- ¼ teaspoon pepper
- 1 tablespoon oil
- 1 bell pepper, chopped
- 1 small onion, chopped
- ½ tablespoon oil
- ½ cup of your favorite barbecue sauce
- 8 ounces Monterey Jack cheese, shredded
- 4 8-inch flour tortillas

For the dipping sauce:

- 1 cup of your favorite barbecue sauce
- ½ cup ranch dressing

1 Preheat oven to 375°F.

2 Line one of the baking sheets with parchment paper. Place the chicken breasts on the parchment paper with at least 2 inches of space between them.

3 Sprinkle salt and pepper on both sides of each breast.

4 Bake the chicken breasts for 25 minutes or until the meat is no longer pink inside.

5 While the chicken is baking, use a skillet to sauté the bell pepper and onion in oil over medium heat until tender. Set aside.

6 When the chicken is done, allow it to cool for about 15 minutes. Then chop the chicken breasts into bite-sized pieces.

7 Turn the oven down to 200°F.

8 Add chicken to the skillet with peppers and onion. Add the barbecue sauce and stir until the ingredients are coated.

9 Add oil to a clean skillet and place one tortilla on the bottom. Put skillet on medium-low heat.

10 Working quickly and carefully, sprinkle on one-fourth of the cheese, leaving about a ½-inch space from the edges.

11 Place half of the chicken and peppers on top of the cheese. Sprinkle another one-fourth of the cheese on top.

12 Add a tortilla and press down firmly. Allow to cook about 1 to 2 minutes or until golden brown. Using a spatula, flip the quesadilla over carefully and cook an additional 1 to 2 minutes.

13 When finished, place on a clean baking sheet in the oven to keep warm while you make the next one.

14 Repeat steps 9 through 12 for a second quesadilla.

15 Slice the quesadillas into wedges and place on a serving platter.

16 Optional: To make a barbecue ranch dipping sauce, measure the barbecue sauce and ranch dressing into a mixing bowl and stir.

CALL AN AUDIBLE

Throwing a grilling football party? These quesadillas are perfect for the grill. Instead of cooking in a skillet, grill the quesadillas over a medium flame for 2 to 3 minutes per side.

SLOPPY JOE NACHO BAR

The second quarter just ended, and your guests are hungry. A Sloppy Joe Nacho Bar will make the perfect halftime show!

PREP TIME	**30** MINUTES
COOK TIME	**30** MINUTES
SERVES	**6 TO 8 PEOPLE**

Tools

- cutting board
- chef's knife
- large skillet
- mixing spoon
- measuring cups/ spoons

Ingredients

- 1 tablespoon oil
- 1 onion, chopped
- 1 red bell pepper, chopped
- 1 green bell pepper, chopped
- 2 cloves garlic, minced
- 2 pounds lean ground beef
- 1 8-ounce can tomato sauce
- 1 cup of your favorite barbecue sauce
- ½ teaspoon dry mustard
- 2 tablespoons Worcestershire sauce
- 1 tablespoon hot sauce
- 1 teaspoon salt
- ½ teaspoon pepper
- 1 12-ounce bag kettle-style potato chips
- 8 ounces cheddar cheese, shredded
- 1 cup bread and butter pickles, roughly chopped
- Optional: 1 cup prepared coleslaw

COACH'S TIP
You never know when some football fans might show up late to the party. Keep the meat warm for your nacho bar by placing it on the warm setting in a slow cooker.

1. In a large skillet, heat the oil on a medium burner. Add the onion, peppers, and garlic. Cook until slightly softened.

2. Add the ground beef and break the meat into chunks using the mixing spoon. Cook over medium heat until no longer pink. With an adult's help, drain the fat carefully.

CALL AN AUDIBLE

If you'd rather move the ground beef to the bench, call in 2 pounds of ground turkey or chicken instead.

3. Add the tomato sauce, barbecue sauce, dry mustard, Worcestershire sauce, hot sauce, salt, and pepper. Turn the heat down to medium-low and simmer for 30 minutes, stirring occasionally.

4. To serve, place chips, meat, cheese, pickles, and coleslaw in separate bowls.

5. Place a layer of chips on each plate, bowl, or container. Then add a couple spoonfuls of meat, followed by cheese, pickles, and coleslaw.

TURKEY ROLL-UPS

Fast and easy finger food is a great way for your guests to eat up without missing any of the football action. They will gobble, gobble down these roll-up appetizers!

PREP TIME 10 MINUTES

COOK TIME 3 HOURS (INACTIVE)

SERVES 6 PEOPLE

Tools

- grater
- cutting board
- spatula
- measuring cup
- plastic wrap
- chef's knife

Ingredients

- 3 burrito-sized flour tortillas
- ½ cup hummus or cream cheese
- 12 slices deli turkey
- 1 cup cheddar cheese, shredded
- 3 romaine lettuce leaves

1 Lay each tortilla flat on a clean surface.

2 Evenly spread the hummus or cream cheese on the tortillas with a spatula. Be sure to go all the way to the edges.

COACH'S TIP

Save time to work on other party chores by prepping the roll-ups the night before. They can safely stay in the refrigerator overnight before slicing.

28

3 Place four slices of turkey on each tortilla, leaving about a ¼-inch border around the edges of the tortilla.

4 Sprinkle ⅓ cup of the cheese on each tortilla.

5 Lay a lettuce leaf on each tortilla.

6 Tightly roll up the tortilla, pressing down on the edges.

7 Place plastic wrap tightly around each roll-up and place in the refrigerator for at least 3 hours.

8 Unwrap tortillas and slice each roll-up into 10 pieces.

9 Place on a serving platter and serve immediately.

PIZZA WAFFLE POCKETS

While you watch your favorite quarterback drop back into the pocket for a pass, grab a breakfast-inspired pocket to enjoy.

PREP TIME	**30** MINUTES
COOK TIME	**10** MINUTES
MAKES	**16** WAFFLE WEDGES

Tools

- waffle iron
- small saucepan
- spoon
- rolling pin
- chef's knife
- measuring cup

Ingredients

- 2 cups marinara sauce
- all-purpose flour
- 2 13.5-ounce packages refrigerated pizza dough
- cooking spray
- 1 cup mozzarella cheese
- your favorite pizza toppings, such as pepperoni, cooked sausage, or sliced veggies

1 Preheat the waffle iron.

2 Place marinara sauce in a small saucepan. Bring to a simmer, then place on low heat and stir occasionally.

3 Sprinkle some flour onto a clean countertop. Split the pizza dough and, using the rolling pin, roll it into four circles that match the size of your waffle iron. If your waffle iron is rectangular, roll the dough into four rectangle shapes.

4 Spray the waffle iron lightly with cooking spray.

5 Place the first circle of pizza dough onto the waffle iron.

CALL AN AUDIBLE

Change your pizza waffle pocket into a classic grilled cheese sandwich! Fill the waffle pocket with grated cheddar cheese instead of mozzarella and pizza toppings. Serve with tomato soup to dip.

6 Sprinkle about one-fourth of the cheese over the dough. Then layer your toppings without overcrowding, followed by another one-fourth of the cheese.

7 Carefully place the second dough circle over the top of the cheese and close the waffle iron. Cook for about 3 to 4 minutes or until golden brown.

8 Remove the waffle and slice into eight wedges. Repeat steps for next batch.

9 Serve with warmed marinara sauce for dipping.

PHILLY CHEESESTEAK SLIDERS

You don't need to be a Philadelphia Eagles fan to fall in love with these sliders!

PREP TIME | **20** MINUTES

COOK TIME | **10** MINUTES

MAKES | **12** SLIDERS

Tools
- large sauté pan
- measuring spoons
- chef's knife
- cutting board
- measuring cup
- large baking sheet
- tongs

Ingredients
- 2 tablespoons olive oil
- 1 small onion, sliced thinly
- 1 bell pepper, sliced thinly
- ½ teaspoon salt
- ¼ teaspoon pepper
- 1 pound flank steak, sliced thinly
- ½ cup beef stock or broth
- 12 slider buns
- 12 slices provolone or Monterey Jack cheese

1 In a sauté pan, heat the olive oil over medium heat.

2 Add the sliced peppers and onions. Cook for about 5 minutes or until slightly softened.

3 Season the meat with salt and pepper on both sides. Carefully add the meat to the skillet without splattering. Stir well.

CALL AN AUDIBLE

For a vegetarian alternative, leave out the beef and beef stock. Instead, add 1 pound of mushrooms to step 2. Skip steps 3 through 5.

4 Add the beef stock or broth and turn the heat up to high.

5 Cook the meat for an additional 1 to 2 minutes or until most of the broth is evaporated. Set aside.

6 Open the slider buns and place them on a large baking sheet.

7 Using a tongs, place an equal amount of meat, onion, and pepper on half of all the buns.

8 Place a slice of cheese on top of the meat and place the pan in the oven.

9 Turn on the oven's broil function. Make sure the oven rack is in the highest position. Broil for about 3 minutes or until the cheese is melted and bubbly. Check often to avoid burning.

10 Place bun tops on the sandwiches and serve.

HAM AND CHEESE PINWHEELS

Team up ham and cheese to set your party spinning with a modern twist on a classic sandwich.

PREP TIME	15 MINUTES
COOK TIME	15 MINUTES
MAKES	ABOUT 16 PINWHEELS

Tools

- large baking sheet
- parchment paper
- mixing bowl
- measuring spoons
- spoon
- bowl scraper
- measuring cup
- chef's knife

Ingredients

- 2 tablespoons cream cheese, softened
- 1 tablespoon Dijon mustard
- 1 sheet frozen puff pastry, thawed
- 4 ounces sliced deli ham
- 1 cup shredded cheddar or Swiss cheese

1 Preheat oven to 375°F and line a large baking sheet with parchment paper. Set aside.

2 In a mixing bowl, combine cream cheese and Dijon mustard, mixing well.

3 Lay out puff pastry on a clean surface. Evenly spread the cream cheese/Dijon mustard mix with a bowl scraper, leaving a ½-inch space at the top of the pastry.

CALL AN AUDIBLE

Experiment with various lunch meats and cheeses. Try roast beef and cheddar or turkey and pepper jack cheese. Go vegetarian by substituting the meat with your favorite sliced vegetables.

4. Layer slices of ham to cover the cream cheese/mustard mix.

5. Evenly sprinkle shredded cheese over the ham.

6. Roll the puff pastry from the bottom to the top.

7. Slice into 16 equal pieces and place on the large baking sheet with about 2 inches between each pinwheel.

8. Bake for 15 to 18 minutes or until golden brown.

9. Allow to cool slightly before serving.

CHOCOLATE-DIPPED FOOTBALL STRAWBERRIES

Your guests will be rushing to get their hands on the ball—sweet and succulent football strawberries, that is!

PREP TIME	**10** MINUTES
COOK TIME	**30** MINUTES
MAKES	ABOUT **25** STRAWBERRIES

Tools

- large baking sheet
- parchment paper
- measuring cup
- 2 microwave-safe bowls
- spoon

Ingredients

- 1 pound strawberries
- 8 ounces semisweet chocolate chips
- 1 0.68-ounce tube decorating gel

CALL AN AUDIBLE

It's easy to make inside-out football strawberries! Substitute white chocolate for the semisweet chocolate, and pipe the laces with brown gel.

1. Wash and pat strawberries dry. Set aside.

2. Line a large baking sheet with parchment paper.

3. Put the semisweet chocolate chips into a bowl. Melt the chocolate chips by microwaving at 10 percent power. Microwave 30 seconds at a time until the chocolate chips are completely melted, stirring in between.

4. Hold the stem of a strawberry and dip into the melted chocolate, as close to the stem as you can. Hold the strawberry above the bowl and allow the excess chocolate to drip off before placing it on the parchment-lined baking sheet. Repeat for all the berries.

5. Place sheet of dipped berries in the refrigerator to harden for about 10 minutes.

6. Leaving the berries on the parchment paper, carefully pipe football laces with the decorating gel onto the chocolate by squeezing the tube.

7. Allow the chocolate and gel to continue to harden for about 30 minutes in the refrigerator before serving.

PEANUT BUTTER BANANA MUFFINS

Peanut butter and bananas team up to make the ultimate flavor combo in these light and fluffy muffins.

PREP TIME	**10** MINUTES
COOK TIME	**30 TO 35** MINUTES
MAKES	**12** MUFFINS

Tools

- muffin tin
- 12 cupcake liners
- measuring cups/ spoons
- saucepan
- spatula
- 2 mixing bowls
- fork

Ingredients

- 4 tablespoons butter
- ¾ cup creamy peanut butter
- 2 cups all-purpose flour
- ½ teaspoon salt
- 1 teaspoon baking soda
- 4 ripe bananas
- ½ cup sugar
- 2 eggs
- ¼ cup milk
- 2 teaspoons vanilla extract

CALL AN AUDIBLE

For an extra-sweet addition, add ½ cup semisweet chocolate chips to the muffin batter in step 5.

1 Preheat oven to 325ºF. Place 12 cupcake liners in a standard muffin tin. Set aside.

2 In a saucepan, melt the butter and peanut butter over medium heat, stirring occasionally. Set aside to cool slightly.

3 In a mixing bowl, add flour, salt, and baking soda.

4 In a second mixing bowl, mash the bananas well with a fork. Then add the sugar, eggs, milk, and vanilla extract. Stir well.

5 Add the banana mixture and the peanut butter mixture to the flour. Use a spatula to scrape the bowl. Stir to combine.

6 Evenly pour the muffin batter into the muffin cups, filling each about ¾ full.

7 Bake for 30 to 35 minutes or until a toothpick inserted comes out clean.

8 Allow to cool 10 minutes before serving.

S'MORES SKILLET

No fireplace? No problem. You don't need a fire to make this delicious treat!

PREP TIME	15 MINUTES
COOK TIME	15 MINUTES
SERVES	8 PEOPLE

Tools
- measuring cup
- medium cast-iron or oven-safe skillet

Ingredients
- 2 12-ounce bags milk chocolate chips
- 2 cups mini marshmallows
- 1 14-ounce box graham crackers, for dipping

CALL AN AUDIBLE

Add some variety to your S'mores Skillet by offering various dipper options, such as vanilla wafer cookies, cinnamon pita chips, or apples.

1 Preheat oven to 450°F.

2 Place the chocolate chips in the bottom of the skillet. Add the marshmallows.

3 Place in oven and bake for 8 to 10 minutes or until the marshmallows turn golden brown. Check often to avoid burning.

4 Carefully remove from oven and serve in the skillet with graham crackers on the side.

CHOCOLATEY FRUITY MINI PIZZAS

Watch your guests start to huddle around you as you hand off tasty dessert mini pizzas.

PREP TIME	15 MINUTES
COOK TIME	15 MINUTES
MAKES	16 MINI PIZZAS

Tools
- mixing bowl
- measuring cup
- bowl scraper
- chef's knife
- cutting board

Ingredients
- 16 sugar cookies, prepared
- ½ cup cream cheese, softened to room temperature
- ½ cup chocolate hazelnut spread
- 1 cup strawberries
- 1 banana
- 2 kiwis
- ½ cup blueberries

CALL AN AUDIBLE

Don't like chocolate? Substitute marshmallow crème or peanut butter for the chocolate hazelnut spread.

1 In a mixing bowl, mix the cream cheese and chocolate hazelnut spread with a bowl scraper.

2 Slice strawberries, banana, and kiwis into bite-sized pieces.

3 Spread about 1 tablespoon of the cream cheese mixture on each cookie with a bowl scraper.

4 Decorate with fruit and serve.

COACH'S TIP

You don't have to stick with the fruits listed here. Get creative! Choose fruits with colors of your favorite teams to show your team pride.

COOKIE BITES

Your guests won't be fumbling these tantalizing, bite-sized cookie bites!

PREP TIME	10 MINUTES
COOK TIME	15 MINUTES
MAKES	25 COOKIE BITES

Tools

- food processor
- measuring cup
- mixing bowl
- spoon
- microwave-safe bowl
- two forks
- large baking sheet
- parchment paper

Ingredients

- 8 ounces of your favorite cookies
- 4 ounces cream cheese, softened to room temperature
- 1 cup white or milk chocolate chips
- decorating icing or gel (optional)

1 Place cookies in the food processor and pulse until the cookies are mostly crumbled. Measure out ¼ cup of the crumbs and set aside. Transfer the remaining crumbs (should be about ¾ cup) to a mixing bowl.

2 Add the cream cheese and mix well. Using a spoon, measure out about 25 pieces. Then roll them in between your palms to make a ball shape. Set aside.

COACH'S TIP

If you don't have a food processor, simply place the cookies in a resealable plastic bag. Press the air out, seal the bag, and pound it with a mallet or rolling pin until you make crumbs.

3 In the microwave, melt the chocolate chips at 10 percent power in 30-second intervals until melted.

4 Using two forks, pinch the ball and drop it in the bowl of chocolate. Roll the ball around until it is covered. Place on a baking sheet lined with parchment paper.

5 After you've dipped all the balls, take the reserved crumbs and sprinkle over the top.

6 Place the baking sheet in the fridge to harden the chocolate for about 30 minutes.

7 Optional: Use decorating icing or gel to create designs or logos.

CALL AN AUDIBLE

While you're rolling the mixture in step 2, shape the balls into helmets instead. Use kitchen shears to cut ropes of licorice into small segments. Attach them to the helmets after step 5 to create face masks.

PEANUT BUTTER CHOCOLATE PRETZEL STICKS

Pretzel sticks are in double coverage! Both peanut butter and chocolate smother the handheld treats.

PREP TIME	10 MINUTES
COOK TIME	15 MINUTES
MAKES	10 PRETZEL STICKS

Tools
- large baking sheet
- parchment paper
- measuring cups
- shallow microwave-safe dish
- bowl scraper

Ingredients
- 1 cup chocolate chips
- ½ cup peanut butter
- 10 pretzel rods
- toppings such as chopped nuts, sprinkles, and shredded coconut

COACH'S TIP
The chocolate might begin to harden in the bowl while you're dipping the pretzels. Instead of fighting through thick chocolate, simply microwave the chocolate for 10 to 15 seconds to melt it again.

1. Line a baking sheet with parchment paper. Set aside.

2. In the microwave-safe dish, melt the chocolate and peanut butter together at 10 percent power in 30-second intervals until melted. Stir to combine.

3. Hold one end of the pretzel rod and dip the other end in the chocolate about two-thirds of the way up the pretzel. You can use a bowl scraper to help apply chocolate to the pretzel.

4. Place on a parchment-lined baking sheet and immediately sprinkle with toppings. Repeat for the remaining pretzel rods. Allow to cool for about two hours before serving.

Three colorful punches provide tasty options to keep your guests from becoming thirsty while cheering during the game!

GINGER-PINEAPPLE PUNCH

Tools

- measuring cup
- punch bowl or large beverage dispenser
- long-handled spoon

Ingredients

- 2 liters ginger ale
- 1 liter pineapple juice
- 1 12-ounce container frozen limeade concentrate, thawed
- ice, for serving

1 In the punch bowl or beverage dispenser, combine the ginger ale, pineapple juice, and limeade concentrate. Stir well.

2 Place in the refrigerator for 3 hours to cool or serve immediately with ice.

CREAMY ORANGE ICE CREAM PUNCH

Tools

- punch bowl
- ice cream scoop
- measuring cup
- long-handled spoon

Ingredients

- 1 pint orange sherbet
- 1 pint vanilla ice cream or frozen yogurt
- 2 liters cream soda
- 2 liters orange soda

TRIPLE-BERRY LEMONADE

Tools
- food processor or blender
- punch bowl or large beverage dispenser
- long-handled spoon

Ingredients
- 1 12-ounce bag frozen berry mix, thawed
- 2 liters lemon-lime soda
- 2 liters ginger ale
- 1 12-ounce container frozen lemonade concentrate, thawed
- ice, for serving

1 Place the berries in the food processor or blender. Blend well.

2 Combine both sodas, lemonade concentrate, and blended berries in the punch bowl or dispenser and stir well.

3 Place in refrigerator for 3 hours or serve immediately with ice.

1 Using the ice cream scoop, place the ice cream and sherbet in a punch bowl.

2 Add the cream soda and orange soda. Stir well before serving.

BRATWURST PRETZEL SLIDERS

Time-out! Are you ready to tackle delicious bratwurst pretzel sliders? Wow your fans with this game-winning recipe.

PREP TIME	**1 HOUR** (30 MINUTES INACTIVE)
COOK TIME	**30 MINUTES**
MAKES	**12 SLIDERS**

Tools

- saucepan
- measuring spoons
- 3 mixing bowls
- measuring cups
- damp kitchen towel
- chef's knife
- large stockpot
- fork
- slotted spoon
- large baking sheet
- parchment paper
- whisk
- pastry brush
- large sauté pan

Ingredients

For the dough:

- 2 tablespoons butter
- 1 packet instant yeast
- 1 pinch of salt
- 1 teaspoon honey
- 1 cup warm water
- 2½ cups flour, plus more for kneading
- vegetable oil spray

For cooking:

- 3 cups water
- ½ cup baking soda
- 1 egg
- 6 fresh bratwurst
- 1 tablespoon olive oil
- 1 onion, thinly sliced
- salt and pepper
- 1 recipe honey-mustard dipping sauce (see page 9)
- sauerkraut (optional)

For the pretzel buns:

1. Place the butter in a saucepan and melt over low heat.

2. In a large mixing bowl, combine the yeast, salt, melted butter, honey, and warm water. Allow to sit for about 2 minutes.

3. Add the flour. Mix it well and turn the bowl of dough onto a floured surface. Knead it well with your hands for about 5 minutes, or until it is soft and smooth.

4 Spray the inside of a clean mixing bowl with vegetable oil spray and place the dough in the bowl. Cover with a clean damp cloth and allow to sit for 30 minutes to rise.

5 Flour your surface again and place the dough ball on it. Knead for 1 minute and then cut the dough into 12 equal pieces.

6 Pour the 3 cups water into the large stockpot. Add baking soda and bring to a boil. Reduce heat to simmer.

7 Sprinkle some flour on a clean counter and roll the dough chunks into balls by rolling the dough in the palm of your hand against the counter. Make sure the dough is smooth all over. Repeat with the remaining dough.

8 Carefully drop four dough balls into the boiling water/baking soda mixture and simmer for about 30 seconds on one side. Then carefully flip using a fork and simmer for an additional 30 seconds. While the dough simmers, line the baking sheet with parchment paper.

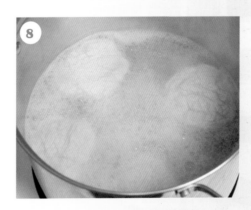

9 Remove the dough with a slotted spoon and place on the parchment paper. Repeat with remaining dough.

10 Whisk the egg in a small mixing bowl. Using a pastry brush, gently paint the top surface of each bun with the egg wash.

11 Carefully score the top of the buns with your chef's knife by marking an X.

12 Sprinkle with salt and bake for 15 to 18 minutes or until the buns are a deep golden brown. Remove and set aside to cool.

13 Slice in half horizontally.

For the bratwurst burgers:

1 Carefully score the casing of the bratwurst lengthwise. Peel the casing off and discard.

2 Cut each sausage link in half. Use your hands to form the meat into 12 patties.

3 Heat olive oil in a large sauté pan over medium heat and add the sliced onions. Stir. Sprinkle a little salt and pepper in the pan. Cook until the onions are softened and slightly golden brown. Remove from pan and set aside.

4 Using the same pan, turn the heat to medium and add the bratwurst patties, working in batches if necessary. Cook for about 3 to 4 minutes per side, or until each side is browned and cooked in the middle.

To assemble:

1 Open the pretzel bun and place a bratwurst burger on the bottom. Add about 2 tablespoons of onion. You can also add sauerkraut on top of the onions.

2 Spread 1 tablespoon of the honey mustard on the inside of the top half of the pretzel bun. Serve on a platter. Now you're cooking like a pro!

SWEET POTATO CHIPS

Instead of cracking open a bag of chips, bring some delicious homemade potato chips to the stadium!

PREP TIME | **10 MINUTES**

COOK TIME | **30 MINUTES**

SERVES | **4 TO 6 PEOPLE**

Tools

- baking sheet
- parchment paper
- chef's knife
- cutting board
- measuring spoons
- 2 mixing bowls
- spatula
- bowl scraper

Ingredients

For the chips:

- 2 medium sweet potatoes
- 1 teaspoon salt
- ½ teaspoon pepper
- 1 teaspoon brown sugar
- ¼ teaspoon cinnamon
- 3 tablespoons olive oil

For the dip:

- 1 chipotle pepper in adobo sauce
- 1 lime
- 1 cup sour cream

1 Preheat the oven to 450°F. Line a baking sheet with parchment paper and set aside.

2 Scrub the sweet potatoes clean and pat dry.

3 Carefully slice sweet potatoes into ¼-inch rounds. Place the rounds in a large mixing bowl.

4 Add remaining ingredients for the chips to the bowl. Toss the ingredients to coat the potatoes with oil and spices.

COACH'S TIP

Find chipotle peppers in adobo sauce in the Mexican food aisle at your local grocery store. They are usually canned or jarred. Save the leftovers in a container in your refrigerator for up to two weeks. Use them in chili, salsa, or any Mexican dish you like!

5 Pour the contents of the bowl on the baking sheet and spread it out. Make sure the potatoes are flat and not stacked on top of each other.

6 Bake for about 15 minutes. Remove the baking sheet from the oven and flip the potatoes over using a spatula.

7 Bake another 15 minutes or until the potatoes are crisp. Remove from the oven and let cool before placing in a bowl for serving.

For the dip:

1 On a clean cutting board, chop the chipotle pepper into very small pieces.

2 Slice the lime in half and squeeze the juice into a small mixing bowl, making sure no seeds fall in.

3 Add the chopped pepper and sour cream.

4 Stir well and place in a small serving bowl alongside the sweet potato chips for dipping.

CHEESY JALAPEÑO CORNBREAD MUFFINS

For an appetizer with a kick, cheesy jalapeño cornbread muffins are a sure crowd-pleaser!

PREP TIME	15 MINUTES
COOK TIME	20 TO 22 MINUTES
MAKES	12 MUFFINS

Tools

- cutting board
- chef's knife
- grater
- 2 mixing bowls
- measuring cups/ spoons
- small saucepan
- spoon
- whisk
- 12 muffin liners
- muffin pan
- toothpick

Ingredients

- 3 tablespoons pickled jalapeños
- 1 cup sharp cheddar cheese
- 1¼ cup finely ground cornmeal
- 1 cup all-purpose flour
- 2½ teaspoons baking powder
- ½ teaspoon salt
- ¼ cup butter
- ⅓ cup honey
- 1 cup buttermilk
- 2 large eggs
- 8 ounces frozen corn

1 Preheat oven to 375ºF.

2 Chop the jalapeños very finely and set aside.

3 Grate the cheddar cheese and set aside.

4 Combine the cornmeal, flour, baking powder, and salt in a mixing bowl.

5 Melt the butter over low heat in the saucepan and set aside.

6 In a second mixing bowl, whisk together the honey, buttermilk, eggs, and melted butter.

7 Pour the liquid ingredients into the dry ingredients and stir until just combined.

8 Stir in the cheese, corn, and jalapeños.

9 Place muffin liners into the muffin pan and scoop batter into the liners. Fill two-thirds full.

10 Bake for 20 to 22 minutes or until a toothpick inserted into a muffin comes out clean.

11 Serve warm or at room temperature.

COACH'S TIP

Make them bite-sized by using a mini-muffin pan! Spray the cups of a mini-muffin pan with cooking spray and fill each three-fourths full. Bake for about 15 minutes or until a toothpick inserted comes out clean.

GRILLED POTATO WEDGES

Ready for a two-minute drill? That's how long it will take for you and your friends to devour these wedges!

PREP TIME	10 MINUTES
COOK TIME	20 MINUTES
SERVES	4 TO 6 PEOPLE

Tools
- 2 mixing bowls
- measuring cups/spoons
- spoon
- cutting board
- chef's knife
- 2 trays or baking sheets
- tongs
- grill

Ingredients
- 3 large baking potatoes
- 1 teaspoon paprika
- 1 teaspoon dried oregano
- 1 teaspoon garlic salt
- ½ teaspoon pepper
- ½ cup olive oil, divided

1 Scrub the potatoes clean and pat dry.

2 Combine the paprika, oregano, garlic salt, and pepper in a small mixing bowl and set aside.

3 Cut each potato into eight pieces by cutting it in half lengthwise. Then cut each half lengthwise again into four wedges.

4 Place potato wedges in a second mixing bowl with half the oil. Toss to coat the potatoes with oil. Place potatoes on a tray or baking sheet and set aside.

5 Heat the grill to 375ºF on one side. If you're using a charcoal grill, move the hot charcoal to one side of the grill. Carefully oil the grill grates with the remaining oil.

CALL AN AUDIBLE

Sub in any firm vegetable for the potatoes, such as sweet potato or zucchini.

COACH'S TIP

If you're worried that your friends will fumble the wedges, put them on a skewer before grilling.

6 Place the wedges on the grill directly over the heat. Cook until browned on all sides for about 2 to 3 minutes per side, using tongs to turn.

7 Once the wedges are browned on all sides, move them to the side without heat. Close the grill for about 10 to 15 minutes or until the wedges are tender.

8 Use tongs to remove the potatoes from the grill. Place on a clean tray or baking sheet and sprinkle on the seasonings. Serve hot.

GRILLED CORN

Listen up! Your friends won't want to pass on these ears. Try out these grilled cobs for the perfect side for your tailgating party.

PREP TIME | **45 MINUTES** (30 MINUTES INACTIVE)

COOK TIME | **20 MINUTES**

SERVES | **6 PEOPLE**

Tools
- large mixing bowl
- saucepan
- cutting board
- chef's knife
- grill
- small mixing bowl
- tongs
- pastry brush

Ingredients
- 6 ears of sweet corn
- water for soaking the corn
- 2 cloves garlic
- ½ stick butter

1 Peel back the husks from the corn but don't remove them. Remove the silk (the stringy stuff inside).

2 Fold the husks back and place the ears in a large mixing bowl with enough water to cover. Let them soak for 30 minutes.

3 Meanwhile, make the garlic butter: Chop the garlic finely and melt the butter in a saucepan over medium heat. Add garlic and let it sizzle until fragrant. Remove from heat right away to avoid burning.

4 Heat grill to 375°F. Put the corn on the grill and cook for about 15 minutes, turning the ears three or four times using tongs.

COACH'S TIP

Avoid burns when removing the husks from the hot corn. Use an old kitchen towel to get a comfortable hold on each ear as you remove the husks after grilling.

5 Use tongs to remove the corn from the grill, but leave the heat on. Remove the husks from the ears of corn. Use a pastry brush to cover the corn with garlic butter.

6 Put the corn back on the grill using tongs. Grill an additional 1 to 2 minutes per side or until some of the kernels are browned. Serve warm immediately.

BAKED BEANS

Shake off the shivers during a chilly fall football game with a piping hot bowl of baked beans.

PREP TIME | **10 MINUTES**

COOK TIME | **1 HOUR**

SERVES | **8 PEOPLE**

Tools

- cutting board
- chef's knife
- sauté pan
- spoon
- measuring cup/ spoons
- 9 x 13-inch baking dish

Ingredients

- 1 small onion
- 3 slices thick-cut bacon
- 1 tablespoon butter
- ¼ cup barbecue sauce
- 2 tablespoons brown sugar
- 1 teaspoon dry mustard
- 2 16-ounce cans pork and beans

1 Preheat oven to 350°F.

2 Chop the onion finely and set aside.

3 Cube the bacon into ½-inch pieces and set aside.

4 In a large sauté pan, heat the butter over medium heat.

5 Add the bacon and onion to the sauté pan. Sauté for about 5 minutes or until the onions have softened slightly. Stir in the remaining ingredients.

6 Pour the contents of the sauté pan into the baking dish.

7 Bake in the oven for about 1 hour and serve warm.

CALL AN AUDIBLE

Vegetarians can skip the bacon! Instead add 1 tablespoon soy sauce for extra flavor.

COACH'S TIP

Try these tips for cutting an onion like a pro! First cut the onion in half from root to end and remove the skin. Place the flat side of the onion on the cutting board and cut several vertical slices evenly across the onion. Don't cut through the root—it will help keep the onion from falling apart. Finally, turn the onion 90 degrees and make slices crosswise.

PRIMAVERA PASTA SALAD

A variety of flavorful ingredients come together in this Pro Bowl salad.

PREP TIME | **30 MINUTES**

COOK TIME | **2 HOURS** (1 HOUR 30 MINUTES INACTIVE)

SERVES | **8 PEOPLE**

Tools

- large stockpot
- measuring cups/ spoons
- chef's knife
- cutting board
- colander
- 2 mixing bowls
- whisk
- bowl scraper
- serving bowl

Ingredients

- 2 tablespoons salt
- 1 pound penne pasta
- 6 spears asparagus
- ½ cup frozen peas
- 3 tablespoons olive oil
- ½ cup cherry tomatoes
- ½ cup grated carrots
- 1 heart of romaine lettuce
- ½ cup olives (optional)

For the sauce:

- ¾ cup plain Greek yogurt
- 3 tablespoons olive oil
- 1 teaspoon lemon juice
- 2 teaspoons garlic, minced
- 2 teaspoons Worcestershire sauce
- ⅓ cup grated Parmesan cheese

1 Fill a large stockpot three-fourths full with water and add salt. Once the water is boiling, add the pasta. Reduce the heat slightly to avoid boiling over. Boil for about 10 minutes or until the pasta is tender but still firm to bite.

2 While the pasta is cooking, chop the asparagus into 1-inch pieces. When the pasta has about 5 minutes left to boil, add the asparagus to the pot. After 3 more minutes, add the frozen peas.

3 Drain the pasta, asparagus, and peas into the colander and run cold water over it to stop the cooking process.

4 Empty the colander into a mixing bowl and drizzle olive oil over the pasta and vegetables. Toss the mixture to coat with oil. Place in the refrigerator to cool while you prepare the other ingredients.

5 Cut the tomatoes in half. Chop the lettuce into bite-sized pieces. Set aside.

6 For the dressing: In a small mixing bowl, combine the yogurt, olive oil, lemon juice, garlic, Worcestershire sauce, and Parmesan cheese.

7 When the pasta and vegetables have cooled, add the tomatoes, lettuce, carrots, olives, and dressing to the mixing bowl. With a scraper, stir to combine the ingredients.

COACH'S TIP

Just like a coach who knows when to sub in the right players, a good chef knows the right balance of ingredients. But sometimes it takes a little experimentation to get it just right. When making the dressing, use more water to thin the dressing if it's too thick. If the dressing is too thin, add yogurt.

8 Pour into a serving bowl, cover, and refrigerate for at least 1½ hours before serving.

HONEY-LIME COLESLAW

Don't leave this tasty coleslaw on the bench! You can put the creamy mixture on burgers, tacos, and sandwiches too.

PREP TIME	**45 MINUTES**
COOK TIME	**1 HOUR** (1 HOUR INACTIVE)
SERVES	**6 PEOPLE**

Tools

- cutting board
- chef's knife
- mixing bowl
- measuring cup/spoons
- whisk

Ingredients

- ½ cup olive oil
- 3 tablespoons honey
- 2 limes, sliced in half
- 1 teaspoon salt
- 1 teaspoon pepper
- 2 teaspoons ground cumin
- ½ small red onion
- 1-pound package coleslaw mix (shredded cabbage and carrots)

1 Make the dressing: Whisk together the olive oil, honey, juice of the limes, salt, pepper, and cumin in a large mixing bowl.

2 Thinly slice the red onion. Add to the mixing bowl.

3 Add coleslaw mix and toss gently to coat.

4 Cover and store in refrigerator for 1 hour before serving.

For a creamier coleslaw, add ¼ cup mayonnaise or Greek yogurt in step 1.

GREEK CHICKEN KABOBS WITH CUCUMBER-DILL YOGURT SAUCE

Fire up the grill for chicken kabobs with a smooth and tangy dipping sauce!

PREP TIME | 1 HOUR 30 MINUTES (1 HOUR INACTIVE)

COOK TIME | 15 MINUTES

SERVES | 4 TO 6 PEOPLE

Tools

- 8 10-inch wooden skewers
- 2 shallow rectangular baking dishes
- measuring cups/ spoons
- 2 mixing bowls
- whisk
- cutting board
- knife
- gallon-sized zip-top bag
- grill
- tongs
- grater

Ingredients

- 1 pound boneless, skinless chicken breasts

For the marinade:

- ½ cup olive oil
- ¼ cup lemon juice
- 1 teaspoon dried oregano
- 1 teaspoon dried rosemary
- 1 teaspoon dried thyme
- 1 teaspoon salt
- ½ teaspoon pepper

For the cucumber-dill yogurt sauce:

- 1 cup plain low-fat or Greek yogurt
- 1 teaspoon dried dill
- 1 tablespoon lemon juice
- ½ English cucumber
- salt and pepper

1 Place the skewers in a shallow baking dish with enough water to cover. Soak for 20 minutes while you prepare the meat and marinade.

2 Place the marinade ingredients in a mixing bowl and whisk to combine. Place the ingredients in the zip-top bag, seal, and set aside.

3 Cut chicken breasts into 1-inch chunks.

4 Place the chicken in the bag and seal. Squish the chicken around in the liquid to cover.

5 Put the bag in a shallow baking dish in the refrigerator. Allow to marinate for at least 1 hour. Marinate for up to 8 hours if preparing ahead of time.

6 After the chicken is done marinating, thread the chicken on the skewers and place in the clean baking dish.

7 Heat the grill to 400ºF. Place skewers carefully on grill for about 5 minutes on each side, or until cooked.

8 Serve with cucumber-dill yogurt sauce.

For the cucumber-dill yogurt sauce:

1 Place the yogurt, dill, and lemon juice in a bowl.

2 Grate the cucumber.

3 Add the cucumber to the bowl and stir well.

4 Add salt and pepper a pinch at a time until it tastes just right.

VEGETABLE KABOBS with HERB RANCH SAUCE

You don't need meat to make a mean kabob! Stack up the veggies and start up the grill for this tailgating treat.

PREP TIME | **1 HOUR 30 MINUTES** (1 HOUR INACTIVE)

COOK TIME | **10 MINUTES**

SERVES | **6 TO 8 PEOPLE**

Tools

- 8 10-inch wooden skewers
- shallow rectangular baking dish
- cutting board
- chef's knife
- tray or baking sheet
- pastry brush
- measuring cups/spoons
- mixing bowl
- bowl scraper

Ingredients

- 1 zucchini
- 2 bell peppers
- 1 small red onion
- 1 pound cherry tomatoes
- ¼ cup olive oil
- 1 teaspoon salt
- ½ teaspoon pepper

For the herb ranch sauce:

- ½ cup plain low-fat or Greek yogurt
- ⅓ cup buttermilk
- ¼ teaspoon garlic powder
- ¼ teaspoon onion powder
- ¼ teaspoon dried thyme
- ¼ teaspoon dried dill
- ½ teaspoon dried parsley
- salt and pepper

1 Place the skewers in the shallow baking dish with enough water to cover. Soak for 20 minutes while you prepare the vegetables.

2 Cut the zucchini in half lengthwise. Then cut into half-moons by cutting across in 1-inch pieces.

3 Cut the peppers in half. Then cut each half into four pieces.

4 Peel and cut the onion in half lengthwise, then widthwise. Peel several layers and set aside.

5 Thread the skewers with zucchini, onions, bell peppers, and tomatoes until the skewers are full. Set the finished skewers on a tray or baking sheet.

6 Using a pastry brush, paint all sides of the vegetables with olive oil, then season with salt and pepper.

7 Heat grill to 400ºF. Carefully place skewers on the grill and cook 3 to 4 minutes per side.

8 Serve with herb ranch dipping sauce.

For the herb ranch sauce:

Combine all the sauce ingredients in a mixing bowl and stir well with a scraper. Allow to sit 10 minutes before serving.

THAI CHICKEN KABOBS WITH PEANUT SAUCE

Get ready to double-dip! Delicious peanut sauce tops off Thai chicken grilled at the stadium.

PREP TIME	**2½ HOURS** (2 HOURS INACTIVE)
COOK TIME	**15 MINUTES**
SERVES	**4 TO 6 PEOPLE**

Tools

- measuring cups/spoons
- 2 mixing bowls
- 2 bowl scrapers
- gallon-sized zip-top bag
- cutting board
- chef's knife
- 8 10-inch wooden skewers
- 2 shallow rectangular baking dishes
- grill
- tongs

Ingredients

- 1 pound boneless, skinless chicken breasts

For the marinade:

- 1 cup plain low-fat yogurt
- ¼ cup soy sauce
- 1 teaspoon turmeric
- 1 teaspoon paprika
- ¼ teaspoon chili flakes

For the peanut sauce:

- ½ cup creamy peanut butter
- 1 tablespoon lime juice
- 2 tablespoons soy sauce
- 2 teaspoons brown sugar
- 1 teaspoon chili-garlic sauce
- ¼ cup hot water

1. Place the skewers in the shallow baking dish with enough water to cover. Soak for 20 minutes while you prepare the meat and marinade.

2. In a mixing bowl, combine the marinade ingredients, stir with the scraper, and pour into the zip-top bag. Seal and set aside.

3. Cut the chicken breasts into 8 strips by cutting lengthwise.

4. Put chicken breasts in the zip-top bag and seal. Squish the bag to coat the chicken.

CALL AN AUDIBLE

Beef up your skewers by replacing the chicken with 1 pound flank steak cut into strips. Cook the steak on the skewers for 3 to 4 minutes per side.

5 Place the bag in a shallow baking dish and refrigerate for 2 hours before grilling.

6 Remove the chicken from the bag and thread the chicken on the skewers. Place the skewers in a shallow baking dish.

7 Heat the grill to 400°F. Carefully place the skewers on the grill and cook about 5 minutes per side, turning with tongs.

8 Serve with peanut sauce.

For the peanut sauce:

1 Combine all the sauce ingredients in a bowl and stir well.

2 Add more hot water to thin the sauce to your liking.

SAUSAGE AND SHRIMP KABOBS WITH HONEY-MUSTARD SAUCE

Stretch out your taste buds in a combination of spicy and tangy with these savory kabobs.

PREP TIME | **15 MINUTES**

COOK TIME | **10 MINUTES**

SERVES | **6 TO 8 PEOPLE**

Tools

- cutting board
- knife
- rectangular shallow baking dish
- 8 10-inch wooden skewers
- tray or baking sheet
- pastry brush
- measuring cups/ spoons
- grill
- tongs

Ingredients

- 1 pound smoked sausage
- 16 shrimp, tails removed
- 1 small red onion
- 2 bell peppers
- ¼ cup olive oil
- 1 teaspoon salt
- ½ teaspoon pepper

For the honey-mustard sauce:

- ½ cup stone-ground mustard
- ¼ cup low-fat yogurt
- ¼ cup honey

1 Place the skewers in the shallow baking dish with enough water to cover. Soak for 20 minutes while you prepare the meat and vegetables.

2 Cut the sausage into 16 1-inch rounds.

3 Cut the sides off of each bell pepper. Then cut each side into four squares.

COACH'S TIP

A clean grill is a safe grill. Dirty grills pose a risk for fire, so make sure you scrub the grates before firing it up.

4 Peel and cut the onion in half lengthwise, then widthwise. Peel 16 layers and set aside.

5 Thread the ingredients onto each skewer in the following order: sausage, onion, shrimp, pepper, sausage, onion, shrimp. Place on the tray or baking sheet.

6 Using the pastry brush, paint the olive oil on the sausage, shrimp, and vegetables on all sides. Use more olive oil if necessary.

7 Sprinkle salt and pepper on all sides.

8 Heat the grill to 400°F. Carefully place skewers on the grill and cook about 3 minutes per side or until shrimp is fully cooked.

9 Serve with honey mustard sauce. To make the honey mustard sauce, simply combine all of the sauce ingredients in a mixing bowl and stir.

BURGER SLIDER

Good (and delicious) things come in small packages!
Watch your friends send in a blitz for these miniature burgers.

PREP TIME	20 MINUTES
COOK TIME	15 MINUTES
MAKES	4 TO 6 PEOPLE

Tools

- cutting board
- chef's knife
- platter or large plate
- mixing bowl
- 2 trays or baking sheets
- grill
- spatula

CALL AN AUDIBLE

Sliders come in many varieties! Sub in ground chicken or pork in place of ground beef. For a vegetarian option, sprinkle the seasonings on portabella mushrooms before grilling.

Ingredients

- 2 pounds lean ground beef
- 1 tablespoon paprika
- 1½ teaspoons salt
- 1 teaspoon pepper
- 1 teaspoon onion flakes
- ¾ teaspoon garlic powder
- 8 slider buns
- your favorite burger toppings, such as cheese, lettuce, sliced tomatoes, onions, pickles, ketchup, or mustard

1. Prepare your toppings and arrange on a platter or large plate. Set aside.

2. Place the ground beef, paprika, salt, pepper, onion flakes, and garlic powder in a mixing bowl.

3. Using your hands, mix the meat well with the seasonings.

4. Separate the meat into eight equal pieces.

5. Form round patties and place on a tray or baking sheet.

6. Heat the grill to 400ºF.

7. Carefully place the patties on the grill and cook about 5 minutes per side or until fully cooked.

8. Transfer cooked burgers to a clean tray or baking sheet.

9. Place the burgers on slider buns, dress with fixings, and serve.

BARBECUED RIBS

Grab some napkins—it's going to get messy! Mouth-watering ribs paired with a savory BBQ sauce make a winning combination.

PREP TIME	10 MINUTES

COOK TIME	5 HOURS 20 MINUTES (5 HOURS INACTIVE)

SERVES	6 PEOPLE

Tools

- measuring cups/ spoons
- small mixing bowl
- cutting board
- heavy-duty aluminum foil
- baking sheet
- grill
- tongs
- pastry brush

Ingredients

- 2 racks baby back ribs, silver skin removed
- 1 cup barbecue sauce, plus more for serving

For the rib rub:

- ²/₃ cup brown sugar
- ¼ cup smoked paprika
- 2 tablespoons pepper
- 1 tablespoon kosher salt
- 1 tablespoon chili powder
- 1 tablespoon garlic powder
- 1 tablespoon onion powder
- 1 tablespoon dry mustard

COACH'S TIP

Know when your ribs are ready to make the transition from oven to grill. Carefully peel back a small part of the rib meat and stick a fork in. If you get no resistance, they're good to go. If it's a little hard to poke the fork in, give them some more time in the oven.

1. Preheat oven to 250°F.

2. Combine the rib rub ingredients in a small mixing bowl and stir to combine.

3. Place rib racks on the cutting board. Sprinkle the rib rub all over the racks, top and bottom.

4. Make foil packets by tearing two sheets of aluminum foil per rack that are slightly longer than the rib racks. Place the ribs on top of the first foil sheet. Then place the second foil sheet over the ribs and seal tightly. Repeat for the second rack of ribs.

5. Put the foil packets on a baking sheet and place in the oven. Bake for about 4 to 5 hours.

6. Heat grill to 450°F. Carefully remove the foil and use tongs to place the ribs on the grill.

7. Use a pastry brush to coat the ribs with barbecue sauce on all sides. Allow to cook for about 5 minutes on each side.

8. Remove the ribs from the grill. Serve immediately with additional sauce on the side.

HAWAIIAN BBQ CHICKEN BURGERS

Aloha! Bring a tropical twist to your tailgating party with these tasty chicken burgers.

PREP TIME | **20 MINUTES**

COOK TIME | **15 TO 20 MINUTES**

SERVES | **6 PEOPLE**

Tools

- mixing bowl
- cutting board
- chef's knife
- measuring cups/spoons
- tray or baking sheet
- grill
- spatula

Ingredients

- 2 pounds ground chicken
- 1 teaspoon paprika
- 1 teaspoon cumin
- 1 teaspoon chili-garlic sauce
- 2 tablespoons soy sauce
- ½ teaspoon garlic powder
- ½ teaspoon salt
- 3 green onions
- oil for brushing on grill grates
- 6 pineapple rings
- 6 slices Monterey Jack cheese
- 6 hamburger buns
- barbecue sauce

1 Combine the ground chicken, paprika, cumin, chili-garlic sauce, soy sauce, garlic powder, and salt in a mixing bowl.

2 Finely chop enough green onions to make one-half cup. Add to the mixing bowl.

3 With your hands, mix the meat lightly with the seasonings and onions.

4 Evenly divide the meat mixture into six pieces. Form the meat into patties and place on a tray or baking sheet.

CALL AN AUDIBLE

Not everyone is a fan of spice! To tame the recipe down a bit, replace the paprika with 1 teaspoon onion powder and the chili-garlic sauce with 1 teaspoon barbecue sauce.

COACH'S TIP

Find chili-garlic sauce in the Asian aisle at the supermarket. It can be used in sauces, marinades, soups, or even as a topping on pizza. Be careful, though—a little goes a long way. It has a kick!

5   Heat the grill to 400°F. Lightly coat the grill grates with oil.

6   Place the patties on the grill and cook 7 to 8 minutes per side or until done.

7   While the patties are cooking, grill the pineapple for 1 to 2 minutes per side. Remove from the grill and set aside.

8   Put cheese slices on the chicken burgers when 1 minute of cooking time remains.

9   Using a spatula, carefully remove the chicken burgers from the grill and place on buns.

10   Place the pineapple on top of the burger and top with barbecue sauce.

11   Add the top bun and serve. Optional: Serve with grilled potato or zucchini wedges (see recipe on pages 58–59).

PULLED CHICKEN TACO BAR

Impress your friends and stifle their hunger by setting up a pulled chicken taco bar right at the stadium!

PREP TIME | **25 MINUTES**

COOK TIME | **4 HOURS** (4 HOURS INACTIVE)

SERVES | **6 PEOPLE**

Tools

- measuring cups/spoons
- 3-quart slow cooker
- cutting board
- chef's knife
- aluminum foil
- small serving bowls and spoons

Ingredients

- 2 pounds boneless, skinless chicken thighs
- 1 15-ounce jar salsa
- 1 tablespoon chili powder
- 1 tablespoon ground cumin
- 1 tablespoon pepper
- 2 teaspoons salt
- 1½ cups cheese, grated
- 2 cups romaine or iceberg lettuce
- 2 tomatoes
- 1 small red onion
- 1 cup sour cream
- additional salsa for topping (optional)
- 12 flour or corn tortillas

1 Combine the chicken, salsa, chili powder, cumin, pepper, and salt in a slow cooker. Stir to combine and cook on low setting for 4 hours.

CALL AN AUDIBLE

If you don't want chicken on your roster, put pulled pork in the game. Use boneless pork shoulder and increase the cook time to 7 to 8 hours.

2 When the meat has 30 minutes left to cook, chop the lettuce and dice the tomatoes and onions. Place the cheese, lettuce, tomatoes, onions, sour cream, and extra salsa in small serving bowls with spoons.

3 When the chicken is done, place it on a cutting board and use two forks to shred the meat. Return to the slow cooker and turn the heat setting to warm.

4 Take slow cooker and toppings to the stadium. Place chicken on tortillas and add toppings.

COACH'S TIP

Taking all those serving bowls to the stadium might be tricky for your tailgating party. Instead, put your toppings in a muffin pan and cover it with foil. Simple to transport and easy to clean!

GRILLED FRUIT ICE CREAM SUNDAES

There's the whistle! It's time for dessert. With this unique sundae, you can combine ice cream and grilling!

PREP TIME	**15** MINUTES
COOK TIME	**15** MINUTES
SERVES	**4** PEOPLE

Tools

- chef's knife
- cutting board
- measuring cups/spoons
- grill
- tongs
- saucepan
- whisk

Ingredients

- various fruits, such as peaches, pineapple, apricots, watermelon, plums, or bananas
- ice cream

For the caramel sauce:

- 2 tablespoons unsalted butter
- ½ cup dark brown sugar
- ¼ cup half-and-half or heavy cream
- ½ teaspoon vanilla extract
- 1 pinch kosher salt

For the chocolate sauce:

- ½ cup semisweet chocolate chips
- ¼ cup low-fat milk
- 1 tablespoon sugar
- 1 pinch salt

1 Slice the fruit into chunks for grilling.

2 To make each sauce, combine the ingredients in a saucepan. Bring to a simmer over medium heat. Reduce to low heat and whisk gently for 5 minutes. Store in separate thermoses to take to the stadium.

3 Heat the grill to 400°F. Grill the fruit for about 3 minutes or until grill marks appear. Use tongs to remove safely.

4 Serve with ice cream and top with the sauce of your choice.

COACH'S TIP

Don't stop with sauces! Add sprinkles, cookie crumbles, or whipped cream to give the sundae your personal touch. Even better, top off your fruit sundae with more fruit—add a cherry!

CARAMEL BROWNIES

Hut! Hut! Hike … one of those brownies in my direction!

PREP TIME | **15 MINUTES**

COOK TIME | **25 TO 30 MINUTES**

SERVES | **8 TO 10 PEOPLE**

Tools

- measuring cups/spoons
- mixing bowl
- scraper
- 8 x 8-inch baking dish
- saucepan
- whisk
- toothpick
- paring knife

Ingredients

- 1 cup flour
- 1 cup sugar
- ½ cup unsweetened cocoa powder
- 1 stick butter, melted
- 2 teaspoons vanilla extract
- 2 eggs
- ¼ cup water
- cooking spray
- 20 soft caramel candies, unwrapped
- ¼ cup sweetened condensed milk

1 Preheat oven to 350ºF.

2 Combine the flour, sugar, cocoa powder, butter, vanilla extract, eggs, and water in a mixing bowl. Stir until most of the lumps of flour are dissolved.

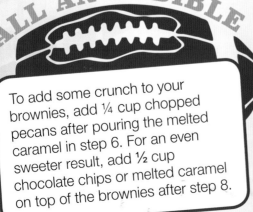

CALL AN AUDIBLE

To add some crunch to your brownies, add ¼ cup chopped pecans after pouring the melted caramel in step 6. For an even sweeter result, add ½ cup chocolate chips or melted caramel on top of the brownies after step 8.

3 Spritz baking dish with cooking spray and pour three-fourths of the batter into the dish.

4 Place in the oven and bake for about 10 minutes.

5 Meanwhile, place the caramels and sweetened condensed milk in a saucepan and whisk slowly over low heat until the caramels melt.

6 Remove the baking dish from the oven and pour the melted caramels over the brownies.

7 Scrape the remaining brownie batter over the caramels and swirl the batter around using the scraper.

8 Return the baking dish to the oven for an additional 25 to 30 minutes or until a toothpick inserted into a brownie comes out clean.

9 Allow to cool for 30 minutes before cutting into squares.

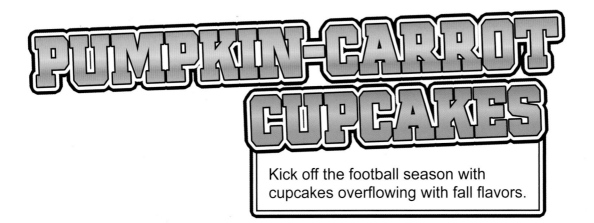

PUMPKIN-CARROT CUPCAKES

Kick off the football season with cupcakes overflowing with fall flavors.

PREP TIME | **15** MINUTES

COOK TIME | **20** MINUTES

MAKES | **12** CUPCAKES

Tools

- muffin tin
- 12 cupcake liners
- 3 mixing bowls
- measuring cups/ spoons
- electric hand mixer
- box grater
- spatula

Ingredients

- 4 tablespoons butter, softened to room temperature
- ½ cup sugar
- 1 egg
- ½ cup canned pumpkin puree
- 1 teaspoon vanilla extract
- ⅓ cup milk
- 1 cup flour
- 1½ teaspoons baking powder
- 1 tablespoon pumpkin pie spice
- ¼ teaspoon salt
- 1 medium carrot
- ½ cup chopped walnuts (optional)

For the frosting:

- 1 8-ounce container cream cheese, softened to room temperature
- 1 cup powdered sugar
- 2 teaspoons vanilla extract

1 Preheat oven to 375ºF.

2 Place 12 cupcake liners in a standard muffin pan. Set aside.

3 In a mixing bowl, combine the butter and sugar. Use an electric hand mixer to blend for about 2 minutes, or until fluffy.

4 Add the egg, pumpkin, vanilla extract, and milk, and mix well.

5 In another mixing bowl, combine the flour, baking powder, pumpkin pie spice, and salt. Set aside.

6 Add the liquid ingredients to the flour mixture. Stir using the hand mixer set on medium.

7 Using a box grater, shred the carrot and add to the mixing bowl. If you want to include walnuts, add them to the mixing bowl as well. Stir to combine.

8 Fill each cupcake liner ⅔ full and bake for 20 minutes or until a toothpick inserted comes out clean.

9 While the cupcakes are baking, make the frosting. In a mixing bowl, combine the cream cheese, powdered sugar, and vanilla extract. Blend with the electric hand mixer until light and fluffy.

10 When the cupcakes are baked, carefully remove them from the muffin tin and allow them to cool completely before frosting.

11 Spread 2 tablespoons of frosting on each cupcake using a spatula.

12 Store in an airtight container until serving.

CALL AN AUDIBLE

Complement these cupcakes' autumn flavors by crumbling ginger snap cookies on top after frosting.

STRAWBERRY SHORTCAKE ON A STICK

What do you get when you cross a classic dessert with a tailgating twist? A sweet shortcake on a stick!

PREP TIME | **10 MINUTES**

SERVES | **8 PEOPLE**

Tools

- cutting board
- paring knife
- chef's knife
- 8 8-inch wooden skewers

Ingredients

- 16-ounce container of strawberries
- 1 pound cake
- 1 7-ounce aerosol can whipped cream

CALL AN AUDIBLE

Mix up the flavor by subbing in different fruits. You can also use cookie cutters to create various shapes with the cake.

1   Cut off the top of each strawberry. Cut the strawberries into ½-inch thick rounds. If the strawberries are between ½ inch and 1 inch, just cut off the tops.

2   Cut the pound cake into four equal sections, lengthwise. Then cut each section into eight squares.

3   Thread one piece of cake onto a skewer, followed by a squirt of whipped cream, then a strawberry. Repeat one to three more times on each skewer. Serve immediately.

PUMPKIN MAPLE WHOOPIE PIES

Give your dessert a double-team of fall flavors! Both pumpkin and maple give these whoopie pies the perfect autumn taste.

PREP TIME	**30** MINUTES
COOK TIME	**15** MINUTES
MAKES	**12** WHOOPIE PIES

Tools

- 2 baking sheets
- parchment paper
- measuring cups/ spoons
- 3 mixing bowls
- whisk
- large spoon
- spatula
- cooling rack
- electric hand mixer
- spoon

Ingredients

- 2 cups all-purpose flour
- 1 teaspoon baking powder
- 1 teaspoon baking soda
- 1 teaspoon ground cinnamon
- ½ teaspoon ground cloves
- ½ teaspoon kosher salt
- 1 stick butter, softened to room temperature
- 1 cup granulated sugar
- 2 large eggs
- 1 tablespoon vanilla extract
- 1 cup canned pumpkin, pureed

For the filling:

- 4 ounces cream cheese, softened to room temperature
- 3 tablespoons butter, softened to room temperature
- ½ teaspoon maple extract
- 2 tablespoons pure maple syrup
- 1 cup powdered sugar
- 1 0.68-ounce tube decorating gel

1 Preheat oven to 350ºF. Line baking sheets with parchment paper and set aside.

2 Combine the flour, baking powder, baking soda, cinnamon, cloves, and salt in a medium-sized mixing bowl. Set aside.

3 Beat the butter and sugar in a large mixing bowl with a whisk for 2 minutes. Add eggs, pumpkin, and vanilla. Beat until smooth.

4 Stir pumpkin mixture into the flour until it's mixed in thoroughly.

CALL AN AUDIBLE

If you don't like maple, you don't have to send this recipe to the locker room. Skip the extract and syrup and use 2 teaspoons of vanilla.

5 Using a large spoon, drop 24 scoops 1 inch apart on the baking sheets. Mold the scoops into ovals.

6 Bake for about 15 minutes.

7 Remove the baking sheets from the oven and allow to cool for 10 minutes. Then use a spatula to transfer the cookies to cooling racks.

8 Meanwhile, make the filling: Using a hand mixer, beat the cream cheese, butter, maple extract, and maple syrup on medium speed in a large mixing bowl until well combined.

9 Add a little powdered sugar at a time while mixing on low speed. After all the sugar is added, turn the mixer up to medium and mix until fluffy.

10 To assemble the whoopie pies, spread a heaping spoonful of filling on the flat side of one cookie. Top it off with another cookie, placing the flat side down. Use the gel to create laces on the top cookie. Repeat with the rest of the cookies.

11 Serve. Store leftovers in an airtight container in the refrigerator.

Whether it's a hot summer day or a cool fall evening, toast the big winners with these tempting tailgating thirst-quenchers.

POMEGRANATE LEMONADE

Tools

- measuring cup
- 2-quart pitcher
- spoon

Ingredients

- 1 quart prepared lemonade
- 1 cup pomegranate juice
- 3 cups seltzer water
- ice

Combine the lemonade, pomegranate juice, and seltzer in pitcher and stir gently. Serve over ice.

RASPBERRY-PINEAPPLE SPRITZER

Tools

- measuring cup
- blender
- 2-quart pitcher
- spoon

Ingredients

- 1 cup raspberries
- 1 quart pineapple juice
- 3 cups seltzer
- ice

Blend raspberries on high until pureed. Combine blended raspberries, pineapple juice, and seltzer in pitcher and stir gently. Serve over ice.

CRANBERRY-APPLE PUNCH

Tools

- measuring cup
- 2-quart pitcher
- spoon

Ingredients

- 3 cups apple cider
- 3 cups ginger ale
- 2 cups cranberry juice
- ice

Combine the apple cider, ginger ale, and cranberry juice in a pitcher and stir gently. Serve over ice.

CREAMY HOT CHOCOLATE

Tools

- 3-quart slow cooker
- measuring cups/ spoons
- whisk
- ladle, for serving

Ingredients

- ½ cup unsweetened cocoa powder
- 1 14-ounce can sweetened condensed milk
- 8 cups milk
- 1 tablespoon vanilla
- 1 teaspoon cinnamon
- marshmallows or whipped cream, for topping

Combine first five ingredients in a slow cooker. Whisk until mostly dissolved. Cook on low for 3 hours. Serve hot with marshmallows or whipped cream.

GRILLED PIZZA

Put away your cell phone! You don't need to order out for pizza at your tailgating party. Prove that you're a cooking pro and create your own pizza combination with a hearty grilled taste.

PREP TIME | **1 HOUR 30 MINUTES**
(1 HOUR INACTIVE)

COOK TIME | **10 MINUTES**

SERVES | **6 PEOPLE**

Tools

- measuring cups/spoons
- 2 mixing bowls
- damp kitchen towel
- cutting board
- chef's knife
- grater
- rolling pin
- pizza stone
- grill
- pizza cutter

Ingredients

For the pizza dough:

- 1 teaspoon active dry yeast
- ½ teaspoon honey
- 1 pinch salt
- ¾ cup warm water
- 1½ cups all-purpose flour, plus extra for kneading
- 1 teaspoon olive oil

For the toppings:

- 1 teaspoon olive oil
- ½ cup pizza sauce
- 1½ cups mozzarella cheese
- 1 teaspoon dried basil
- your favorite toppings, such as pepperoni, cooked sausage, ham, mushrooms, onions, peppers, pineapple, or cheddar cheese

For the dough:

1 In a large mixing bowl, add the yeast, honey, salt, and water. Stir once thoroughly and allow to sit for about 10 minutes or until all of the ingredients have dissolved and bubbled.

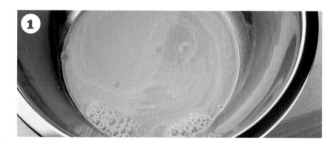

2 Add flour to the bowl and use your hands to mix the ingredients well.

3 Sprinkle some flour on a clean surface and put the dough ball on it. Knead until the dough is soft and smooth, about 8 to 10 minutes. Add more flour to the surface if it starts to get too sticky.

4 Coat the inside of the second mixing bowl with the olive oil. Place the dough ball in the bowl and cover with a damp towel. Allow to rise for about an hour.

5 Meanwhile, get your toppings ready. Grate the cheese. Slice the meats and vegetables thinly so they cook quickly when the pizza is grilled. Set the toppings aside.

6 After the dough has finished rising, sprinkle flour on a flat surface. Place the dough in the flour. Give it a quick knead—just one or two times. Then put some flour on the rolling pin and roll the dough into the shape of the pizza stone. Coat the pizza stone with olive oil and place the dough on top of it.

7 Spoon the pizza sauce on the dough, using the back of the spoon to spread it to ½ inch from the edge.

8 Sprinkle about three-fourths of the cheese on top of the sauce. Place your toppings on the cheese. Be careful not to overload the pizza, or it may get soggy! Then add the rest of the cheese and the dried basil on top of the pizza.

Go outside the playbook and make a white pizza! Instead of pizza sauce, drizzle ¼ cup olive oil and 1 teaspoon crushed garlic on the pizza dough before you pile on cheese and your favorite toppings.

9 Heat the grill to 450°F. Place the stone on the grill and close the lid. Grill for 8 to 10 minutes or until the crust is slightly browned and the cheese is bubbly.

10 Use the pizza cutter to slice into triangles and serve.

MAPLE NUT GRANOLA CEREAL

It's the day of the big game! Although the kickoff doesn't happen for hours, you'll want to start fueling your body in the morning. Start off by making granola with a maple-nut crunch. You can eat it as cereal with milk or mix it with yogurt.

PREP TIME | **10 MINUTES**

COOK TIME | **45 MINUTES**

MAKES | **8 TO 10 SERVINGS**

Ingredients

- 2 cups rolled oats
- ½ cup walnuts, chopped
- ⅓ cup ground flaxseed
- ½ cup raisins
- ½ cup pure maple syrup
- ⅓ cup olive oil
- 2 teaspoons maple extract
- ⅛ teaspoon salt

Tools

- baking sheet
- parchment paper
- mixing bowl
- measuring cups/ spoons
- spoon

1 Preheat oven to 300°F and line a baking sheet with parchment paper and set aside.

2 In a mixing bowl, combine the oats, walnuts, flaxseed, and raisins.

3 Add the remaining ingredients. Gently stir until the oats are well coated.

4 Spread the mixture evenly on the baking sheet.

5 Bake for about 45 minutes or until slightly browned.

6 Allow to cool completely, then break into chunks.

7 Store leftovers in an airtight container for up to two weeks.

ATHLETE NUTRITION

Go nuts over the walnuts in this cereal! Not only are they tasty, but they provide all-important iron. This essential mineral helps carry oxygen in your blood and to your muscles.

COACH'S TIP

Have fun with your granola!
Spread 2 tablespoons
peanut butter on a slice
of apple for a tasty treat.
Then sprinkle granola on top.

PUMPKIN WAFFLE SANDWICH

Ready for a breakfast sandwich that will help you keep your eyes on the ball? Pumpkin contains plenty of vitamin A to keep your vision sharp on the field.

PREP TIME | **10** MINUTES

COOK TIME | **5** MINUTES

MAKES | **4** WAFFLE SANDWICHES

Tools

- 3 mixing bowls
- measuring cups/ spoons
- whisk
- waffle iron
- tongs
- spoon
- knife

Ingredients

- ½ cup all-purpose flour
- 1 teaspoon baking powder
- 1 teaspoon pumpkin pie spice
- 1 pinch salt
- 1 egg
- 3 tablespoons pure maple syrup
- ¼ cup canned pureed pumpkin
- ½ cup milk
- 1 tablespoon canola oil
- cooking spray

For the filling:

- 3 tablespoons cream cheese, softened to room temperature
- ½ teaspoon maple extract

1. In a mixing bowl, combine the dry ingredients: flour, baking powder, pumpkin pie spice, and salt.

2. In a second mixing bowl, whisk the wet ingredients: egg, syrup, pumpkin, milk, and canola oil until smooth.

3. Gently add the wet ingredients to the dry ingredients. Stir to combine.

4. Heat a waffle iron, and spritz with cooking spray.

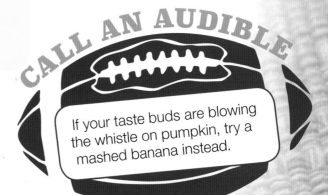

CALL AN AUDIBLE

If your taste buds are blowing the whistle on pumpkin, try a mashed banana instead.

5 Pour half the batter on the iron. Cook according to the waffle iron directions or until golden brown and slightly crispy on the outside.

6 Remove from the iron using tongs and repeat with the second half of the batter.

7 For the filling, combine the cream cheese and maple extract in a small mixing bowl and stir until smooth.

8 When both of the waffles are done, spread the cream cheese on one of the waffles and place the second on top to make a sandwich.

9 Cut into quarters and serve.

SCRAMBLED EGG MUFFINS

After a game or workout, protein helps build and repair your muscles. Lucky for you, these muffins have scrambled eggs, which are high in protein!

PREP TIME | **10 MINUTES**

COOK TIME | **20 MINUTES**

MAKES | **4 EGG MUFFINS**

Tools
- muffin tin
- measuring cup
- mixing bowl
- whisk
- chef's knife
- cutting board

Ingredients
- cooking spray
- 2 eggs
- ¼ cup milk
- 1 pinch salt
- 1 pinch black pepper
- 2 slices deli ham
- ½ red bell pepper
- ¼ cup grated cheddar or Swiss cheese

1 Preheat oven to 350ºF. Spritz cooking spray in four cups of a standard muffin tin and set aside.

2 Beat the eggs, milk, salt, and pepper in a mixing bowl and set aside.

3 Dice the ham and red pepper into small pieces.

4 Add the cheese, ham, and red pepper to the eggs and mix.

5 Evenly pour the mixture into the muffin cups.

6 Bake for about 20 minutes or until the eggs are cooked through. The eggs are done when they are slightly firm but not hard.

7 Cool for about 5 minutes before serving.

CALL AN AUDIBLE

Vegetarians can eject ham from the recipe and put in some of their favorite veggies. Try the recipe with mushrooms, zucchini, or onions.

APPLE-CRANBERRY OATMEAL

This easy and delicious oatmeal provides your body with plenty of complex carbohydrates. They are a great source of long-lasting energy for your game day!

PREP TIME | **10 MINUTES**

COOK TIME | **10 MINUTES**

MAKES | **1 SERVING**

Tools
- cutting board
- chef's knife
- saucepan
- measuring cups/spoons
- spoon

Ingredients
- 1 apple
- 1 cup rolled oats
- 2 cups milk
- 3 tablespoons dried cranberries
- 2 tablespoons pure honey

1 Dice the apple into bite-sized pieces and set aside.

2 In a small saucepan, combine the oats and milk and place on a stovetop at medium heat.

3 Bring to a simmer and stir frequently.

4 As the oats soften, add the apple, cranberries, and honey.

5 Continue to stir for about 5 minutes. Serve warm.

CALL AN AUDIBLE

Add more toppings to your oatmeal. Toss in some chopped nuts for added crunch and flavor. You can also combine recipes by adding some Maple Nut Granola Cereal from page 100.

What are complex carbohydrates and why are they good for your body? Complex carbohydrates are made of several sugar molecules. They provide long-lasting energy and stabilize your blood sugar, which boosts your endurance. Complex carbohydrates are also high in vitamins, minerals, and fiber.

GRILLED HAM AND CHEESE QUESADILLAS WITH TOMATO BISQUE

Carbohydrates, proteins, fats, and fiber work to keep our bodies running smoothly. You'll find all of them in this delicious and nutritious balanced meal.

PREP TIME | **15 MINUTES**

COOK TIME | **30 MINUTES**

MAKES | **4** 1-CUP SERVINGS OF SOUP AND **2** QUESADILLAS

Tools

- cutting board
- chef's knife
- saucepan
- measuring cups/spoons
- spoon
- large skillet
- spatula
- plate
- blender

Ingredients

For the soup:

- 1 small onion
- 1 clove garlic
- 1 15-ounce can crushed tomatoes
- 1 12-ounce can vegetable broth
- 1 teaspoon dried basil
- ½ cup half-and-half
- 1 teaspoon salt
- ½ teaspoon black pepper

For the quesadillas:

- 1 cup cheddar cheese, grated
- 6 slices deli ham
- 1 tablespoon olive oil
- 4 medium whole-wheat flour tortillas

1 Start with the soup: Chop the onion into small pieces and mince the garlic. Place the onions and garlic, along with the tomatoes, broth, and basil, in a medium-sized saucepan on a stovetop with medium heat.

COACH'S TIP

Be careful when blending hot liquids. Hot steam builds pressure and can make the lid burst off, causing a big mess or burns. To prevent a cooking disaster, work in batches and only fill your blender half full. Always be careful when you take the lid off.

2 Stir to combine until it begins to bubble. Reduce the heat to medium-low and simmer for 10 minutes.

3 Meanwhile, chop the deli ham into bite-sized pieces. Set aside.

4 Place the oil in a large skillet over medium-high heat until it begins to sizzle.

5 Put one tortilla in the pan. Quickly and carefully sprinkle a quarter of the cheese on the tortilla, followed by half of the ham.

6 Add another quarter of the cheese, followed by a second tortilla, forming a sandwich. Allow to cook for about 1 to 2 minutes or until golden brown.

7 Using a spatula, carefully flip the quesadilla over and cook an additional 1 to 2 minutes.

8 Move the quesadilla from the pan to a plate and repeat steps 5 through 7 with the other two tortillas.

9 Cut the quesadillas into wedges and set aside while you finish the soup.

10 Carefully transfer the soup to a blender. Blend until smooth.

11 Return to the saucepan and add the half-and-half, salt, and pepper. Stir to combine.

12 Serve soup hot with quesadillas on the side.

STRAWBERRY-WALNUT CHICKEN SALAD

Go green with this sweet and savory salad! The mixed greens will give your vitamin A intake a boost.

PREP TIME | **15 MINUTES**

COOK TIME | **10 MINUTES**

MAKES | **2 CUPS**

Tools

- skillet
- measuring cups/ spoons
- plate
- spoon
- chef's knife
- cutting board
- 2 mixing bowls
- whisk
- 2 forks

Ingredients

- ¼ cup walnuts
- 1 tablespoon pure honey
- 1 pinch salt
- 3 strawberries
- 4 slices red onion
- 1½ cups mixed baby greens
- ½ cup rotisserie chicken, sliced

For the dressing:

- 4 tablespoons raspberry yogurt
- 1½ tablespoons red wine vinegar

ATHLETE NUTRITION

Vitamin A does more than keep your vision sharp. It also helps keep your immune system strong and prevents you from getting sick—so you can stay in the game!

CALL AN AUDIBLE

Not a nut fan? Make croutons instead! Cut a slice of bread into 1-inch cubes and place them on a baking sheet. Then drizzle 1 tablespoon of olive oil and sprinkle a pinch each of salt and pepper over the bread. Bake in the oven at 400°F for about 10 minutes or until golden brown.

1. In a skillet, combine the walnuts, honey, and salt. Place over medium-high heat, stirring frequently for about 2 to 3 minutes. Remove from heat and place the nuts on a plate to cool.

2. Cut the tops off the strawberries. Slice the strawberries into quarters and set aside.

3. Cut the onion into ¼-inch slices and set aside.

4. In a large bowl, combine the walnuts, strawberries, red onion, mixed greens, and chicken.

5. Make the dressing: In a small mixing bowl, whisk the yogurt and vinegar until smooth.

6. Drizzle the dressing over the salad and toss lightly with two forks to coat the salad. Serve in a bowl.

PITA PIZZA

Pizza on a game day? That's right! Start off with a pita instead of regular pizza crust and build your own tasty creation.

PREP TIME	**10** MINUTES
COOK TIME	**10** MINUTES
MAKES	**1** PIZZA

Tools
- chef's knife
- cutting board
- baking sheet
- measuring cup/spoon
- pizza cutter

Ingredients
- 1 whole-wheat pita pocket
- 2 tablespoons pizza sauce
- ½ cup mozzarella cheese, grated
- your favorite pizza toppings, such as peppers, onions, mushrooms, ham, pepperoni, pineapple, or spinach

1 Preheat oven to 425°F.

2 Chop toppings into small pieces and set aside.

3 Spread pizza sauce on the pita pocket, followed by the cheese and toppings.

4 Place on a baking sheet and bake for 5 to 10 minutes, or until the cheese is bubbly and melted.

5 Remove from oven and slice into wedges with the pizza cutter. Allow to cool for 2 minutes. Serve hot.

COACH'S TIP
Choose your toppings wisely! By using a variety of ingredients, you can cover many food groups in your Pita Pizza.

BLT WRAP

Toast is so second-string! Use a tortilla to wrap up the classic ingredient trio before you head to the field.

PREP TIME	**5** MINUTES
COOK TIME	**10** MINUTES
MAKES	**1 WRAP**

Tools

- skillet
- tongs
- paper towels
- cutting board
- chef's knife
- measuring spoons
- small mixing bowl
- spoon
- toothpicks

Ingredients

- 2 slices bacon
- 1 small tomato
- 1 tablespoon ranch dressing
- 1 teaspoon Dijon mustard
- 1 10-inch whole-wheat flour tortilla
- 2 romaine lettuce leaves

CALL AN AUDIBLE

If bacon's not a star player on your team, feel free to sub in sliced turkey or ham in its place.

COACH'S TIP

Don't want to deal with splattering bacon on the stove? Cook your bacon in the oven on a baking sheet at 375°F for 15 to 20 minutes or until crispy. You can also cook the bacon in a microwave, although it won't get as crispy. On a microwave-safe plate, place two paper towels, the bacon strips, and then two more paper towels. The bacon should not overlap. Cook for about 2 minutes.

1. In a skillet over medium heat, cook the bacon until crisp—about 5 minutes on each side, using tongs to turn. Place on a paper towel to drain.

2. Cut the tomato into four slices and set aside.

3. Combine the ranch dressing and Dijon mustard in a small mixing bowl. Spread evenly on the tortilla.

4. Place the bacon on the tortilla, followed by the tomato and lettuce.

5. Roll up tightly and secure with toothpicks.

6. Slice in half and serve.

YOGURT PARFAIT

As you layer on your gear and uniform, dig through the fruit and yogurt layers of this parfait.

PREP TIME | **5 MINUTES**

MAKES | **1 PARFAIT**

Tools

- measuring cups
- cutting board
- chef's knife
- bowl
- spoon
- tall glass or parfait glass

Ingredients

- ¼ cup raspberries
- ¼ cup blueberries
- ¼ cup strawberries
- 1 cup of your favorite yogurt
- ¼ cup Maple Nut Granola Cereal (see page 100)

1 Cut the strawberries into small pieces.

2 Mix the strawberries with the raspberries and blueberries in a bowl and set aside.

3 In a tall glass or parfait glass, add ⅓ cup of the yogurt, followed by ½ of the berry mixture. Repeat the layers, ending with the yogurt.

4 Top with granola and serve cold.

CALL AN AUDIBLE

You don't have to stick with just raspberries, blueberries, and strawberries. Mix and match your favorite fruits! Peaches, pineapple, and bananas can add a flavor twist to your parfait. If you want more crunch, mix some of the granola into the berry layers.

POPCORN TRAIL MIX

Mix it up and stay satisfied! For an energy boost that will help carry you through the game, grab a handful of this sweet and salty combo.

PREP TIME | **10** MINUTES

COOK TIME | **3** MINUTES

MAKES | **3** CUPS

Tools

- paper lunch bag
- measuring cups/spoons
- 2 mixing bowls

Ingredients

- ½ cup popping corn kernels
- 1 teaspoon coconut or olive oil
- ¼ teaspoon salt
- 1 cup roasted almonds
- 1 cup roasted peanuts
- ½ cup pumpkin seeds
- ½ cup semisweet chocolate chunks
- ½ cup raisins

COACH'S TIP

Use single-serve zip-top bags to portion out the trail mix. Then you'll be set for a tasty snack every day of the week!

1 In a mixing bowl, combine the popping corn, oil, and salt. Stir until well coated.

2 Place the mixture into the paper lunch bag. Fold the top of the bag down two times to seal.

3 Place upright in a microwave. Cook on high for 2 minutes or until you no longer hear the corn popping for 1 or 2 seconds.

4 Allow to cool before opening the bag. Be careful—steam might escape out of the bag!

5 Combine the remaining ingredients and the popcorn in a second mixing bowl and stir well.

6 Transfer to an airtight container or large zip-top bag to store leftovers for up to one week.

VANILLA-ALMOND POWER BARS

The perfect treat to snack on during halftime! This granola bar will give you a boost of energy for the second half.

PREP TIME	**30** MINUTES
COOK TIME	**10** MINUTES (INACTIVE)
MAKES	**12** BARS

Tools

- baking sheet
- parchment paper
- saucepan
- measuring cups/spoons
- spoon
- mixing bowl
- knife

Ingredients

- ¼ cup canola oil
- ½ cup pure honey
- ¼ cup creamy peanut butter
- 2 teaspoons vanilla extract
- 2½ cups rolled oats
- 1 cup puffed brown rice cereal
- 1 cup chopped roasted almonds
- ½ cup chopped roasted peanuts
- ½ cup semisweet chocolate chips

1 Line the baking sheet with parchment paper and set aside.

2 In a medium-sized saucepan, combine the canola oil, honey, peanut butter, and vanilla extract over medium-high heat. Stir until it begins to simmer. Reduce heat to low and cook for about 3 minutes. Set aside.

3 In a large mixing bowl, combine the oats, rice cereal, almonds, peanuts, and chocolate chips.

CALL AN AUDIBLE

You can swap out three ingredients if you'd rather send the nuts to the bench! Sub in sunflower butter for the peanut butter. To keep the crunch, use lightly crushed pretzels instead of almonds and peanuts.

4 Pour the mixture from the saucepan into the mixing bowl and stir until the oats are well coated.

5 Press the oats firmly into the baking sheet, packing the mixture tightly.

6 Refrigerate for at least an hour before cutting into bars. Store leftovers in an airtight container.

ATHLETE **NUTRITION**

Did you know a peanut isn't really a nut? It's a legume—in the same group as peas and beans. Peanuts and peanut butter are packed with lots of fiber and protein that serve as a source of fuel for your energy and muscles.

CHEESY CRACKERS

For a quick halftime snack, grab a handful of these protein-rich crispy crackers.

PREP TIME | **10 MINUTES**

COOK TIME | **30 MINUTES**

MAKES | **100 CRACKERS**

Tools

- box grater
- cutting board
- measuring spoons/cups
- food processor
- plastic wrap
- baking sheet
- parchment paper
- rolling pin
- pizza cutter
- toothpick

Ingredients

- 1 8-ounce block sharp white cheddar cheese
- 4 tablespoons butter
- 1 cup whole-wheat flour plus extra for rolling
- 1 teaspoon salt
- ¼ teaspoon black pepper
- ¼ teaspoon cayenne pepper
- 3 tablespoons milk

1 Grate the cheese. Use the side of the grater that has fine holes.

2 Combine the cheese and butter in the food processor with the blade attachment.

3 Place the cover on and turn on low until the cheese and butter make small crumbles.

4 Turn off and add the flour. Turn the power back to low for about 15 seconds.

5 With the processor off, add the milk. Then turn the power on low one last time for about a minute or until the dough forms a ball. It should be slightly sticky.

6 Shape into a flat disc and cover in plastic wrap. Refrigerate for at least an hour.

7 Preheat oven to 375°F and line a baking sheet with parchment paper. Set aside.

COACH'S TIP

Have fun with your crackers! Use mini-cookie cutters to create fun shapes before you put the dough in the oven.

8 Sprinkle a couple pinches of flour on a clean counter. Roll the dough with a rolling pin until it is about 1/8-inch thick.

9 Use a pizza cutter to cut into squares. Poke a hole into the center of each cracker with a toothpick.

10 Place on the baking sheet and bake for about 30 minutes or until just golden.

11 Allow to cool before serving. Store leftovers in an airtight container for up to a week.

FRUIT KABOBS

An easy way to eat the rainbow! Share this fruity snack with your teammates for a burst of vitamin C.

PREP TIME	15 MINUTES
MAKES	12 KABOBS

Tools

- chef's knife
- cutting board
- 12 10-inch wooden skewers

Ingredients

- 24 strawberries
- 1 cup pineapple
- 1 cup cantaloupe
- 4 kiwis
- 1 cup blueberries
- 1 cup green grapes

ATHLETE NUTRITION

Feeling a slump at halftime? Fruit provides lots of energy through natural sugars. Fruit contains a lot of water, which helps prevent dehydration. The vitamin C helps your body recover during the game.

1. Start by prepping the fruit. Cut the tops off the strawberries. Cut the pineapple into 1-inch chunks. Cut the cantaloupe into ½-inch slices. Peel and slice the kiwi into ½-inch rounds.

2. Thread each skewer with the strawberries, cantaloupe, pineapple, kiwi, blueberries, and grapes. Get creative with your order of fruit!

3. Store in an airtight container or large zip-top bag in a refrigerator or cooler with ice packs until serving.

CALL AN AUDIBLE

Switch up the taste of your kabobs by changing the lineup of fruit. Mix and match the fruit from the ingredient list with watermelon chunks, orange segments, apples, honeydew, or red grapes.

MIXED BERRY ICE POPS

Your team won the game! Celebrate with delicious ice pops that will cool down you and your teammates.

PREP TIME	**10** MINUTES
COOK TIME	**4 HOURS** (INACTIVE)
MAKES	**6** ICE POPS

Tools

- measuring cups/spoons
- blender
- ice pop form

Ingredients

- 2 cups low-fat plain yogurt
- 2 cups frozen mixed berries
- ½ cup 100 percent apple juice
- 1 teaspoon vanilla extract
- 2 teaspoons honey

CALL AN AUDIBLE

Sub out the flavors to get a new take on the ice pops. Try 2 cups frozen mangoes in place of berries and ½ cup 100 percent pineapple juice instead of apple juice for a tropical twist.

1 Place ingredients in a blender.
Blend until smooth.

2 Pour the mixture evenly in
an ice pop form.

3 Place the top of the form on and
freeze for 4 hours before serving.

COACH'S TIP

Don't have an ice pop form?
No problem! Make mini-ice pops
by using an ice cube tray. Pour
the mixture evenly into the cube
cups and place in the freezer for
1 hour. Remove from the freezer
and stick one toothpick into each
cube. Put back in the freezer for
2 hours before serving.

CHOCOLATE-BANANA SMOOTHIE

Recover from a grueling game with this healthy alternative to a chocolate-banana milkshake.

PREP TIME | **10 MINUTES**

MAKES | **1 SMOOTHIE**

Tools

- cutting board
- chef's knife
- blender
- measuring cups/spoons

Ingredients

- 1 peeled banana, frozen
- 1 cup milk or almond milk
- ¼ cup low-fat plain yogurt
- 1 teaspoon vanilla extract
- 2 tablespoons unsweetened cocoa powder

ATHLETE NUTRITION

After a practice or game, it's important to replenish your body. Bananas contain simple carbohydrates, which are fast-acting sugars that go into recovery mode to rebuild and restore muscles. Other fruit to eat post-game are raisins, blueberries, grapes, watermelon, or pears.

1. Cut the banana into 1-inch rounds and place in the bottom of a blender.

2. Add the remaining ingredients.

3. Blend until smooth and serve immediately.

COACH'S TIP

The more ripe the banana, the sweeter it'll taste. Freeze bananas that are almost too ripe to eat. They'll last up to three months in the freezer and be ready for smoothies.

SOUTHWEST BLACK BEAN QUINOA BOWL

A satisfying post-game meal will restore your muscles with this south-of-the-border-inspired dish.

PREP TIME | **15 MINUTES**

COOK TIME | **20 MINUTES**

SERVES | **4 2-CUP SERVINGS**

Tools

- measuring cups/ spoons
- mesh strainer
- 2 saucepans
- cutting board
- chef's knife
- can opener
- skillet
- spoon

Ingredients

- 1 cup quinoa
- 2 cups water
- 1 red bell pepper
- 1 small red onion
- 1 tablespoon olive oil
- 1 teaspoon salt
- 2 teaspoons cumin
- 2 tablespoons lime juice
- ¼ teaspoon cayenne pepper
- 1 15-ounce can sweet corn, drained
- 1 15-ounce can black beans, drained

Garnishes:

- grated cheddar cheese, sour cream, salsa, diced avocado, chopped scallions, and lime

1. Rinse the quinoa by placing in a mesh strainer and running cool water over it. Place in a saucepan with 2 cups water and bring to a boil.

2. Reduce the heat to low and cover. Cook for 15 to 20 minutes or until all the liquid is absorbed.

3. Meanwhile, slice the red pepper and onion into bite-sized pieces.

4. Heat oil in a skillet over medium heat. Add peppers and onions, along with salt, cumin, lime juice, and cayenne pepper. Cook 5 to 6 minutes or until slightly softened.

5. Add corn and black beans to the skillet. Stir until heated.

6 Combine the cooked quinoa with the veggies and stir to combine.

7 Serve in bowls and top with desired garnishes.

CALL AN AUDIBLE

Add some extra protein to your lineup! Shred 2 cups rotisserie chicken and add it to your quinoa bowl.

FISH TACOS

Fish is the ultimate athlete fuel. It provides a healthy balance of nutrition to help you recover faster and reduce soreness after the game.

PREP TIME | **30 MINUTES**

COOK TIME | **5 TO 10 MINUTES**

MAKES | **6 TACOS**

Tools

- cutting board
- chef's knife
- 2 mixing bowls
- measuring spoons
- shallow baking dish
- skillet
- tongs

Ingredients

For the mango salsa:

- 1 mango
- 1 tomato
- ½ bunch cilantro
- 1 teaspoon salt
- ½ teaspoon pepper

For the tacos:

- 1 pound firm white fish, such as cod
- 1 tablespoon lime juice
- 1 tablespoon olive oil
- 1 tablespoon cumin
- 1 teaspoon salt
- ¼ teaspoon cayenne pepper
- 6 flour tortillas
- garnishes such as sour cream, grated cheese, and lettuce

1 Chop the mango and tomato into small pieces. Place in a mixing bowl.

2 Chop the cilantro finely and add to the bowl, followed by the salt and pepper.

3 Stir well and place in the refrigerator while you cook the fish.

CALL AN AUDIBLE

Not a fan of seafood? Replace the fish with chicken. For a vegetarian option, chop 1 pound of your favorite vegetables, such as bell peppers, onions, mushrooms, or zucchini, to use in place of the fish.

4 Cut the fish into 2-inch cubes and place in a shallow baking dish.

5 In a small mixing bowl, combine the lime juice, olive oil, cumin, salt, and cayenne pepper. Whisk well and pour over the fish. Allow to marinate for 5 minutes.

6 In a skillet over medium heat, add the fish and marinade. Using tongs, carefully turn the pieces over after 3 minutes. Then cook another 3 to 4 minutes or until cooked through.

7 Evenly place fish on six tortillas, followed by mango salsa and desired garnishes. Serve immediately.

COACH'S TIP

How do you know if your fish is done? Check by pressing your tongs gently against the piece of fish. If it flakes, it's done. If the meat is resistant, try cooking another minute or two and check again.

VEGETABLE PASTA

Bring on the whole wheat and pour on the veggies with this healthful pasta that will recharge you after the game.

PREP TIME | **20** MINUTES

COOK TIME | **20** MINUTES

MAKES | **4** 2-CUP SERVINGS

Tools

- stockpot
- colander
- cutting board
- chef's knife
- skillet
- measuring cups/spoons
- can opener
- spoon
- tongs

Ingredients

- 1 tablespoon salt
- ½ pound whole-wheat pasta
- 1 yellow bell pepper
- 1 small onion
- ½ cup olive oil
- 1 cup frozen broccoli florets
- 3 teaspoons garlic, minced
- 1 15-ounce can fire-roasted tomatoes
- 1 teaspoon black pepper
- 1 tablespoon lemon juice
- ¼ cup Parmesan cheese, shaved

1 Fill a large stockpot ¾ full with water and add 1 tablespoon salt. Bring to a boil and cook pasta according to package directions. Drain and set aside.

2 Meanwhile, chop the bell pepper and onion into small pieces.

3 In a skillet, heat oil over medium heat and add zucchini and onions. Cook until slightly softened, stirring occasionally. Add broccoli and garlic and cook an additional 2 to 3 minutes.

4 Add tomatoes, pepper, and lemon juice. Reduce heat to low.

CALL AN AUDIBLE

For a little extra flavor in your pasta, add sliced summer squash in step 3 and sliced cherry tomatoes in step 5.

5 Combine the vegetables with the pasta in the skillet and toss together using tongs.

6 Serve in bowls and sprinkle with cheese.

STUFFED TURKEY BURGERS

You don't have to wait until Thanksgiving to stuff a turkey! These burgers are filled with cream cheese, mozzarella, and roasted red peppers.

PREP TIME	15 MINUTES
COOK TIME	15 MINUTES
MAKES	4 BURGERS

Tools

- chef's knife
- cutting board
- measuring cups/ spoons
- 2 mixing bowls
- nonstick skillet

Ingredients

- ¼ cup roasted red peppers
- 4 tablespoons cream cheese, softened to room temperature
- ¼ cup mozzarella cheese, shredded
- 2 pounds ground turkey
- ¼ cup bread crumbs
- 1 egg white
- 2 teaspoons salt
- 1 teaspoon black pepper
- ½ teaspoon garlic powder
- ½ teaspoon onion powder
- 4 whole-wheat hamburger buns
- toppings such as lettuce, tomato, ketchup, or pickles

1 Using a chef's knife, chop the roasted red pepper into ¼-inch cubes and place in a mixing bowl. Add the cream cheese and mozzarella, and stir to combine.

2 In a second mixing bowl, add the turkey, bread crumbs, egg white, salt, pepper, garlic powder, and onion powder. Mix well with your hands.

3 Form eight thin patties and place on a clean cutting board.

COACH'S TIP

To separate the egg white to use in the recipe, take a small bowl and place it on a counter or table. Hover one of your hands slightly above the bowl, with your palm facing up. Gently crack the egg and open it into your hand over the bowl. Allow the egg white to slip between your fingers until only the yolk is left in your palm.

4 Evenly scoop the cream cheese mixture on four of the patties.

5 Place a bare patty on top of a patty with cream cheese. Press along the edges to create a seal. Make three more with the other six patties.

6 Heat a nonstick skillet over medium heat.

7 Carefully place the patties in the skillet and cook about 7 minutes on each side, using a spatula to flip them.

8 Remove from pan and serve on hamburger buns with toppings.

ATHLETE NUTRITION

Turkey is a great alternative to beef, especially for athletes. It has a similar amount of protein but much less fat so you can build muscle without adding inches.

SALMON WITH COUSCOUS SALAD

Your body needs to refuel after the game, and salmon—with couscous on the side—will bring you back up to speed.

PREP TIME | **10 MINUTES**

COOK TIME | **1 HOUR 10 MINUTES** (1 HOUR INACTIVE)

MAKES | **4 SERVINGS**

Tools

- saucepan
- measuring cups/ spoons
- fork
- cutting board
- chef's knife
- mixing bowl
- mixing spoon
- skillet
- tongs

Ingredients

For the couscous salad:

- 1 cup whole-wheat couscous
- 1½ cups vegetable broth
- 1 tablespoon olive oil
- 2 teaspoons garlic, minced
- 1 cup cherry tomatoes
- 1 small cucumber
- 1 small red onion
- 1 tablespoon fresh basil
- ¼ cup Parmesan cheese, grated
- ¼ teaspoon salt
- 1 teaspoon black pepper

For the salmon:

- 4 6-ounce salmon fillets
- 1 teaspoon salt
- 1 teaspoon black pepper
- 1 tablespoon olive oil

1. First make the salad: In a saucepan, combine the couscous, vegetable broth, olive oil, and garlic. Bring to a boil and remove from heat. Then cover and allow to sit for 5 minutes or until the liquid is absorbed. Remove the lid and fluff the couscous with a fork by stirring it a few times. Allow to cool slightly.

2. Slice the tomatoes in half. Then cut the cucumber, onion, and basil into small pieces.

3. In a mixing bowl, combine the couscous, tomatoes, cucumber, onion, basil, Parmesan cheese, salt, and pepper. Stir well and place in a refrigerator to cool for an hour.

4. Evenly sprinkle the salt and pepper on both sides of the fish fillets.

5 In a skillet, heat oil over medium-high heat and add fillets. Cook about 4 to 5 minutes per side, or until the fish is cooked through.

6 Serve immediately with the couscous salad.

INSIDE-OUT CHICKEN PARMESAN

If you've mastered the other recipes, you're ready to prove you're a pro in the kitchen! Impress your friends by turning the classic chicken Parmesan dish inside-out!

PREP TIME	20 MINUTES
COOK TIME	30 MINUTES
MAKES	4 SERVINGS

Ingredients

- 4 boneless, skinless chicken breasts
- 4 slices mozzarella cheese
- 4 tablespoons Parmesan cheese, grated
- 1 bunch fresh basil
- 1 teaspoon salt
- 1 teaspoon black pepper
- 2 tablespoons olive oil
- 1 28-ounce jar marinara sauce
- 1 pound whole-wheat pasta
- 1 tablespoon salt

Tools

- cutting board
- plastic wrap
- mallet
- 4 plates
- measuring spoons
- toothpicks
- shallow baking dish
- stockpot
- colander
- tongs

1 Cover the cutting board with plastic wrap.

2 Put a chicken breast in the center of the cutting board. Then place another piece of plastic wrap over the chicken. Press it flat to make a seal.

3 Using a mallet, gently pound the chicken breast until it is evenly flat and about ½-inch thick. Remove the chicken from the plastic and set on a clean plate.

COACH'S TIP

You don't need to throw in the towel if you don't have a mallet. A small heavy-bottomed pan will work in a pinch.

4 Repeat steps 2 and 3 for the other three breasts. Then remove the plastic wrap from the cutting board.

5 Put one breast on the cutting board. In the center of the breast, place 1 slice of mozzarella cheese, 1 tablespoon of Parmesan cheese, and 4 basil leaves.

6 Fold the sides of the breast in and roll it up, like a burrito. Secure the chicken with toothpicks so it stays tightly rolled. Set aside.

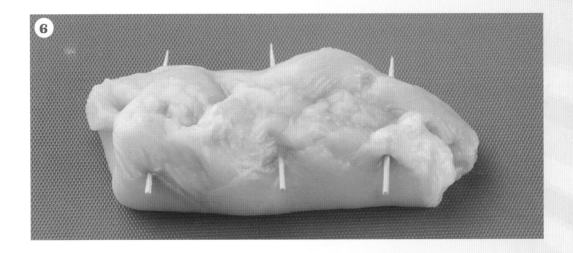

7 Repeat steps 5 and 6 for the other three breasts.

8 Preheat oven to 375°F.

9 Place the chicken breasts evenly apart in the shallow baking dish. Sprinkle with salt and pepper. Bake in the oven for 35 to 40 minutes or until the chicken is cooked through.

10 Meanwhile, fill a stockpot ¾ full of water and add 1 tablespoon salt. Bring to a boil.

11 Cook pasta according to package directions and drain in a colander.

12 Pour marinara sauce into the stockpot over medium heat. Bring to a simmer, then reduce heat to low.

13 When the chicken is done, carefully remove the toothpicks.

14 Add the pasta to the marinara sauce and toss carefully.

15 Serve by placing the pasta on a plate with the chicken breast on top.

Sports Illustrated Kids' Football Cookbooks are published by Capstone Press,
1710 Roe Crest Drive, North Mankato, Minnesota 56003.
www.capstonepub.com

Library of Congress Cataloging-in-Publication Data
Jorgensen, Katrina, author
  Food, football, and fun! : sports illustrated kids' football recipes /
by Katrina Jorgensen.
      pages cm.—(Capstone young readers)
  Summary: "A football cookbook with recipe ideas for a football party,
tailgating, and fueling up for game day"—Provided by publisher.
  Audience: Ages 9-15.
  Audience: Grades 4 to 6.
  Includes bibliographical references.
  ISBN 978-1-62370-230-4 (paperback)
1. Outdoor cooking—Juvenile literature. 2. Tailgate parties—Juvenile
literature. 3. Parties—Juvenile literature. 4. Snack foods—Juvenile
literature. I. Title.
  TX823.J668 2015
  641.5'78—dc23   2014034094

Editorial Credits
Anthony Wacholtz, editor; Kyle Grenz, designer;
Eric Gohl, media researcher; Laura Manthe, production specialist;
Marcy Morin, scheduler; Sarah Schuette, food stylist

Photo Credits
All images by Capstone Studio: Karon Dubke; author photo by
STILLCODA Photography.

About the Author

Katrina Jorgensen is a graduate of
Le Cordon Bleu College of Culinary Arts.
She enjoys creating new recipes and
sharing them with friends and family.
She lives in Rochester, Minnesota,
with her husband, Tony, and dog, Max.

Printed in China.
042015   008869RRDF15